Spiritual

Growth

Revised Edition

Don Clowers

Spiritual Growth (Revised Edition)
ISBN 0-9639956-1-8
Copyright © 1995, 2002 by Don Clowers

Contents

Foreword

The Bible says, **That the God of our Lord Jesus Christ, the Father of glory, may give unto you the spirit of wisdom and revelation in the knowledge of him: The eyes of your understanding being enlightened; that ye may know what is the hope if his calling, and what the riches of the glory of his inheritance in the saints** Ephesians 1:17,18.

Don Clowers has been a tremendous blessing to my life, and I believe as you read this book you will understand why. He unveils the basic truths of the Bible and breaks them down for practical application in your everyday Christian walk. You will receive a wealth of wisdom as you read every page...from why your words affect you and your circumstances, to what the Bible has to say regarding giving.

It's not your shouting on Sunday that will help you weather the storms of life but how you walk throughout the week when faced with the reality of everyday circumstances. My prayer is that as you read this book, your life will be forever ...**changed into the same image** (of the Lord) **from glory to glory, even as by the Spirit of the Lord** 2 Corinthians 3:18.

Rod Parsley
Pastor
World Harvest Outreach

Preface

As I update this book it is the year 2002 and I am in my 44th year of ministry. Looking back over these years, I can recall many things God did to help me grow in my spiritual walk.

I also remember mistakes I have made. I now realize that most of these mistakes could have been avoided had I received proper training and instruction at an early stage in my Christian walk.

This brings me to the reason I wrote this book. I wanted to provide a guide to the steps in Christian maturity in order to help the reader avoid many of the mistakes others (including myself) have made. As a guide, this book will answer questions you may have and will serve as a reminder of things you already know.

I have experienced disappointments, problems, and pains in the course of my life, but I continue to mature and develop as a Christian by applying God's Word to my daily life. As you prayerfully read this book I pray that the Holy Spirit will motivate you to begin to apply all these God-given principles to your life.

Ultimately, it is my prayer that this book will help you see that you can be an overcomer in all things…that you can become all that God intends for you to be…and that you can deal effectively with anything that comes your way!

May God bless you and guide you and enlighten you as you move ahead on your journey to spiritual growth.

Don Clowers

Introduction

A newborn Christian can be compared to a tiny baby. There is a definite parallel between the two. A baby is born into this world with all the physical organs and body parts that he or she will ever need for a lifetime. These body parts, however, are immature and a process of growth begins to take place. With even the most basic nourishment, the physical body will grow to adult stature.

This is not true for the mind. If there is no stimulation, there is no growth. The capacity is there, but a lack of knowledge can hinder the fulfillment of a person's potential.

The same is true of a person who becomes born again. When he accepts Jesus as his Savior, the new life of God comes into his spirit.

Therefore if any man be in Christ, he is a new creature: old things are passed away; behold, all things are become new. 2 Corinthians 5:17

At the moment of being born again, all of God's love is there, all of God's power is there. The supernatural potential is there, but a new convert must learn how to walk daily in this power and use it. The source of God is in the recreated spirit. The spirit is reborn instantly, but the mind must be renewed to God's way of doing things.

Some people expect newborn Christians to be able to stand alone spiritually. This is a grave mistake. When a person is born again, whether it is in church, at a Bible Study, on a bus, over the phone, or in the street, the believer should obtain the convert's name, address, and phone number. The convert can then be directed to a place where discipling can take place—where there is a teaching of the uncompromised gospel of Christ. Believers can be encouragers to the new convert in this new walk.

Imagine a mother putting her infant child to bed, handing the bottle to the baby, and saying: "Feed yourself." Imagine her putting diapers in the crib and saying: "Change yourself." What a ridiculous notion! The mother understands that even though the baby has hands, there is no understanding or ability to use them. Therefore, she gladly holds the bottle for her baby and changes the diapers when necessary.

The mother can be heard saying cute things to the baby. The words might seem senseless to a listener, but she is communicating love by the tone of her voice and the expression on her face. She does not speak to the child as she would to an adult. In fact, she doesn't even expect the baby to respond—except with a few gurgles and maybe a brief smile.

This same concept applies to new Christians. Like newborn babies, they need to be nurtured. They cannot be expected to do the things that mature Christians do. They must be given time to grow up and mature; the same way a baby is given time to grow up and mature. Of course, it will not take as much time for the convert to grow up as it does the natural child. But that growth will depend on how much love, care, and proper teaching the convert receives from mature sisters and brothers in the Lord.

Often we are guilty of saying to a convert, "If you're really saved, you'll come to church and grow up." Instead, we should make the effort to love new converts and share with them. They need attention and instruction. As a mother and father look after their child, we should do the same with a newborn child of God. With good instruction and nurturing the convert will, little by little, learn to do things independently. He must be taught to pray, meditate, read the Word of God, go to church regularly, give of his time and give of his substance.

My wife Sharon and I believe that we were loving and patient parents. We were loving, yet firm, with our four children. Tammy was our first child. We noticed everything she did. We encouraged her to sit up, crawl, and take her first steps. As she tried to walk, we helped steady her until she gained confidence in her own ability to take steps on her own.

When Tammy was ten months old, Sharon bought her a training cup. She told me that when Tammy became eleven months old, she was going to take her bottle away. She began teaching Tammy to drink from her training cup. The day Tammy was eleven months old, Sharon took the bottle from her. Tammy had no difficulty making this transition because she had already been learning to use the training cup and had developed the technique of drinking from it.

Such systematic, careful training is just as necessary for new converts. People who are born again have made the decision to accept Jesus Christ. They made that decision on their own. Mature believers must, in turn, train them and then encourage them to take further steps on their own to grow up spiritually.

Without the proper help and environment, some believers never grow to spiritual maturity. They become carnal Christians and their walk with God is like a child who goes through life with physical and mental problems and is always having a difficult time. They never know the real joy of serving the Lord. They live a life of defeat rather than victory.

My hope and prayer is that as you read this book, the Holy Spirit will teach you, encourage you and enlighten you and that you will experience new understanding of God's ways…that you will be motivated to move forward with God and experience the blessings of spiritual growth…

Chapter 1
The Natural Man

But the natural man receiveth not the things of the Spirit of God: for they are foolishness unto him: neither can he know them, because they are spiritually discerned.

1 Corinthians 2:14

A person who has never been born again is referred to in this scripture as the "natural man." That person cannot understand the things of God because God's life is not in him or her. The natural man is motivated by worldly things and ruled by Satan. This is not referring to demon possession, but to the fact that the light of God has not come into the unsaved person's spirit. The god of this world, Satan, exercises control over unregenerated spirits.

But if our gospel be hid, it is hid to them that are lost: In whom the god of this world hath blinded the minds of them which believe not, lest the light of the glorious gospel of Christ, who is the image of God, should shine unto them.

2 Corinthians 4:3,4

Paul is saying here that the person who has not accepted Jesus is in darkness and is blinded to the things of God. He learns and experiences everything through the five senses: hearing, seeing, tasting, smelling, and feeling. The Christian, on the other hand, has a different method of learning and receiving knowledge—he learns by the Spirit of God.

The spirit of man is the candle of the Lord, searching all the inward parts of the belly.

Proverbs 20:27

In the miracle of the new birth, God's Spirit unites with the spirit of that convert. When the new Christian goes to church, hears and reads the Word of God and meditates on it, understanding comes as to how the Word of God is spiritually discerned or understood.

Long-time church goers have told me that for years they served on the board of deacons, or taught Sunday School, or sang in the choir, yet they did not know Jesus as personal Savior. As a result, the service was only a form or an act—it was not genuine. It could not be genuine until Jesus became the Lord of their lives.

A good friend of mine—a church pastor—is a classic example. He attended church for two years, and during that time he became an elder and taught Sunday school. Yet, by his own admission, he had no personal relationship with Jesus Christ.

He said, "I was not even born again; I had never asked Jesus into my life. I didn't know anything about the Bible, yet I taught a Sunday school class." When I asked him what he taught, he told me he taught a form of God because he did not know God.

Satan, who is the god of this evil world, has made him blind, unable to see the glorious light of the Gospel that is shining upon him...

2 Corinthians 4:4 (TLB)

My friend's eyes had been blinded to spiritual things. We cannot begin to understand the spiritual things of God until His life is part of ours. He confessed that his favorite part of church was the dismissal prayer. Why? Because what he was doing was merely a form and he was bored.

His wife grew up in a different spiritual environment and she continually witnessed to him. Other people outside his church also witnessed to him. Finally, his eyes were opened to the truth that he was practicing a form of religion. As a result, he became dissatisfied with the direction of his life and one day he accepted Jesus Christ as Lord and Savior of his life.

After his life was transformed and he received the baptism in the Holy Spirit, he had to go to another place of worship to have fellowship. He could not stay where he had been because they did not teach the things of God by experience. They only taught *about* God. There is a big difference!

This gentleman now pastors a successful Full Gospel Church and teaches people how to be born again by the Spirit of God.

Attending church isn't enough

It's a shame that people are deluded to think everything is all right simply because they attend church. The truth is that without God our wisdom is earthly or natural.

But if ye have bitter envying and strife in your hearts, glory not, and lie not against the truth. This wisdom descendeth not from above, but is earthly, sensual, devilish.

James 3:14,15

The natural man's wisdom is not from God. James says that person is motivated by selfishness, jealousy, envy, and strife. The daily life of an unsaved person is filled with frustration, fear, and bitterness.

It's disturbing to think that churches are led by people who have never let Jesus come into their lives. How can those who have never received Jesus help and encourage others in the things of God? Churches led by people who are not born again become mere social gatherings because the gospel is hidden. They are blinded from true revelation of God. It becomes a case of the "blind leading the blind." This is not said to be critical of others, but rather to open our eyes to pray for them.

The natural man obeys the passion of the senses, carries out the dictates of the flesh and follows the prince of the power of the air. That person is obedient to Satan and under his control, walking in the course of this world. There is no inward life from God because he is led by his feelings.

And you hath he quickened, who were dead in trespasses and sins; Wherein in time past ye walked according to the course of this world, according to the prince of the power of the air, the spirit that now worketh in the children of disobedience: Among whom also we all had our conversation in times past in the lusts of our flesh, fulfilling the desires of the flesh and of the mind; and were by nature the children of wrath, even as others.

Ephesians 2:1-3

Paul says here that an unsaved person follows the devil because he or she by nature is a child of wrath and disobedience. Because the inner person is filled with darkness, conversations and thoughts are of the world. He is not interested in the things of God and seeks after worldly pursuits.

Jesus first – then growth and change

Many people are turned off to God because they are told all the things they must stop doing when they become Christians. This is not the best approach to use to win a person to Jesus Christ. I grew up in a strict Pentecostal Church. Because I was afraid of God, I ran away from Him instead of running to Him. I went to church and was told all the things I was not allowed to do. These strict rules prevented me from receiving a picture of a loving and kind God.

Women were told they could not cut their hair, use makeup or wear slacks. I was told I could not go swimming in public or go to the movies. My impression was that accepting Jesus into my life meant giving up good times. When I did pray, it was due to fear of going to hell, not because of my love for God.

The time came when I made a quality decision to serve the Lord because I wanted to. When this happened, there was a joy in serving Him! Of course, I didn't want to go to hell—neither should anyone—but that should not be the only reason to come to Christ. How much better to come to Him because we hunger for His love, His life and His wisdom. When a person comes to Him because of a deep desire of the heart, it's a real commitment!

God accepts us as we are—no matter what we have done. The answer is not to discontinue doing things, but to accept what Jesus has done for us. He comes into our hearts when we accept Him as Lord—and He doesn't hold anything against us!

We need not try to change people. That's God's job. When a person accepts Jesus, the old things pass away and all things become new. The change in our spirits comes immediately—but the change in our minds comes perpetually. It's like fishing—we must first catch the fish before we can clean it! Christians are sometimes guilty of trying to clean up potential converts and then get them saved. But the first step is to lead them to accepting Jesus as Lord; then as they grow and revelation is received, they will put away earthly or worldly things.

> **Once you were less than nothing; now you are God's own. Once you knew very little of God's kindness; now your very lives have been changed by it.**
>
> **1 Peter 2:10 (TLB)**

Life without Jesus has no real purpose because there is nothing to hold on to. Once we are changed by the grace of God, we not only have a purpose and a reason to live for today, but we also have the hope of our eternal existence with Jesus Christ when He comes after His Church.

Chapter 2
The Carnal Christian

The fact that a Christian is carnal does not mean he or she is not born again. The carnal Christian may be a new convert who is just beginning to grow. Or it could be someone who has been saved for many years but is still a baby in the things of God. He accepted Jesus years ago but made no effort to develop and mature in spiritual matters. That person chooses to be fed with milk instead of meat. The flesh rules and there is no indication of a daily trusting in God.

I have said that newborn Christians should be helped, directed, loved and encouraged by other believers. The time comes, however, when the convert is ready to take steps on his own. Just as my wife Sharon took the bottle from each of our four children, new Christians need to break away from total dependence on other believers and the pastor.

Abraham and Sarah had a feast on the day that Isaac was weaned and put on solid food. It was a time to celebrate (Genesis 21:8). It should be the same way with Christians as they begin to grow and are no longer controlled by their fleshly desires. They learn to walk by faith and not by sight (2 Corinthians 5:7). It is a time to celebrate because they are putting the old things behind and are learning to live victoriously.

Carnal Christians may speak in tongues occasionally, but they still act in many ways as though they were not saved. They have not renewed their minds to the things of God. Their church attendance and tithing patterns are inconsistent. They may be touchy, depressed, and discouraged and they fail to experience the prosperity that God has for them.

> **However, brethren, I could not talk to you as spiritual [men], but as to non-spiritual (men of the flesh, in whom the carnal nature predominates), as to mere infants [in the new life] in Christ—unable to talk yet!**
> **I fed you with milk, not solid food, for you were not yet strong enough [to be ready for it],**
> **For you are still (unspiritual, having the nature) of the flesh—under the control of ordinary impulses. For as long as [there are] envying and jealousy and wrangling and factions among you, are you not unspiritual and of the flesh, behaving yourselves after a human standard and like mere (unchanged) men?**
> **1 Corinthians 3:1-3 (AMP)**

Notice that Paul addressed the carnal people as "brethren." He said he could not talk to them like spiritual adults, but had to talk to them as though they were babies in the Christian life. They are men and women who follow not after the things of God, but after their own fleshy desires. Paul told them they were acting like people who didn't belong to the Lord at all. When Christians are jealous of one another, compete against one another, quarrel, find fault, and want their own way, they are clearly displaying their stage of growth.

One may say, "I am a follower of Paul," another says, "I am follower of Apollos." This again reveals they are living as ordinary (mere) men.

Who are you following?

Carnal Christians are followers of personalities more than they are followers of God's character in a person. When something causes them to lose confidence in the person they are following, they also tend to lose confidence in the things that person has taught from God's Word.

On the other hand, balanced Christians have confidence in ones who are used of God, but do not go overboard. They see that God is in those who are ministering the Word, yet they will go back to the scriptures to see if what they are being told is from God.

And ye became followers of us, and of the Lord…
1 Thessalonians 1:6

We should show respect, trust, and confidence in the one who is ministering the Word. We must also keep our eyes on Jesus, the author and finisher of our faith.

Carnal Christians are controlled by their feelings

Some carnal Christians will go to church, but they never apply what they are learning to their lives. Some quote and confess the Word and may even seem spiritual, but when attacks from Satan come they give in to their feelings. They are very touchy and as a result cry and feel sorry for themselves. They often say, "I just don't understand why this is happening to me." They become frustrated, discouraged, depressed and mope around for days at a time.

Ever learning, and never able to come to the knowledge of the truth.
2 Timothy 3:7

Actually they know what to do, but they refuse to take God's Word and do it. Their immaturity shows through any spiritual front they might hide behind. Remember, a carnal Christian is not necessarily a newborn

Christian, but is one who at any chronological stage of Christianity refuses to grow up and develop in the things of God.

Excuses

There are some carnal Christians who continually use excuses for not doing the things of God. You may tell them to pray and meditate in the Word, but they have an excuse for not doing so. They have an excuse for not coming to church regularly. They always have a "good" reason to keep from making any real commitment to the body of Christ. A carnal Christian is unpredictable. One may go to church, another may not. Most pretend to be very spiritual. One thing is sure—they remain in infancy stages.

Self-control

But the fruit of the Spirit is love, joy, peace, longsuffering, gentleness, goodness, faith, meekness, temperance; against such there is no law.

Galatians 5:22,23

The fruit of the Spirit is love. It is received at the moment of the new birth. It is imparted to our spirits. It is within our treasure chests. It is deposited into our account to write checks on! But we must take self-control and develop the fruit of the Spirit every day—in all circumstances. Joy, peace, longsuffering, gentleness, goodness, faith, meekness and temperance must be developed. It is all there in love, but if we don't use self-control and draw the love from within us, we will remain immature Christians.

We must take responsibility for our actions. We can take each day and make it a good one. We've all heard the saying: "Have a nice day." But very seldom do we *have* a nice day—it's up to us to *make* it a nice day. Each day is filled with circumstances, some good and some not so good.

Consequently, we must exercise patience. We must be joyful. We must be kind when we don't feel like being kind. We must give when we don't feel like giving. We must be faithful when we don't feel like being faithful. We must model our attitude after the attitude of Jesus in all things.

Be renewed in the attitude of your mind.

Ephesians 4:23 AP

Some years ago I was invited to speak at a Pentecostal church. As I began speaking, I noticed a group of people sitting near the middle of the church. Most of the time they sat with their heads down. When they did look up, the expressions on their faces were terrible. This went on for some time. Then all of them got up and walked out. On their way out, one of them spoke out disapprovingly, "Worldliness!"

I continued to speak as though nothing had happened. After the meeting was over I asked the pastor, "Do you know the people who walked out?"

"Oh yes," he said, "they are some of my best members."

I then replied, "Apparently I said something that offended them. Do you know what it could have been?"

He told me that it was nothing I had said.

"What was it then?" I asked.

A look of embarrassment crossed his face. He stammered a moment, then said, "It's your hair."

At that time my hair was over my ears and they evidently felt that it was too long. They were calling me worldly because my hair was over my ears. However, they were the ones who were worldly because they did not use self-control, nor did they show the God-kind of love in their actions. Even if I had been wrong, their immaturity was indicated by the type of attitude they manifested toward me.

Chapter 3
The Spiritual Man

When I was a child, I spake as a child, I understood as a child, I thought as a child; but when I became a man, I put away childish things. 1 Corinthians 13:11

When I was a child, one of my favorite pastimes was pretending with my older brother. We would tie the ends of a rope around our waists and he pulled me with it. We were pretending to be a tractor and trailer. Even though I enjoyed this, we normally got into an argument because I tired of being the trailer. Sometimes I wanted to be the tractor. My brother usually got his way because he was older.

I liked to sit in my dad's car and pretend to drive, or pretend that I was the pilot of an airplane. But I was just a child, acting and responding as a child should. As I began to mature, I put away childish things. I did not pretend any longer; I became of age. I obtained a driver's license and drove a car.

Paul was saying this same thing. At one time in his life, he was a child. He reasoned and understood as a child until he became a man. At that point he put away childish things. The same is true of the spiritual Christian. When we are mature Christians, we put away the old life and walk in the spiritual realm. We are not controlled by the flesh, but rather by the Spirit of God. Not only are our actions controlled by the Spirit of God, but also our reactions. In emergency situations, or when there is bad news or symptoms, the mature Christian does not act or react as the carnal Christian would. The Christian who walks according to the Spirit stands in the strength of the Word of God and is not moved by circumstances.

The Word of God has first place in the life of the mature believer. Meditation in the Word is a priority, as is a consistent prayer life. As a result, he or she thinks godly thoughts, has the mind of Christ, and walks in godly wisdom. That person is a winner and knows that God has made a way of escape.

> **There hath no temptation taken you but such as is common to man: but God is faithful, who will not suffer you to be tempted above that ye are able; but with the temptation also make a way to escape, that ye may be able to bear it.**
>
> **1 Corinthians 10:13**

> **For he hath made him to be sin for us, who knew no sin; that we might be made the righteousness of God in him.**
>
> **2 Corinthians 5:21**

Knowing our righteousness

Truly knowing our righteousness can be the most powerful force in our lives. When we know we are in right standing with God, we know we have God's ability. All fear and inferiority are gone and have been replaced with the confidence and boldness to do God's will, to live as Jesus lived and to manifest greater works in our lives than He did! We cannot earn righteousness—*it is a gift!*

The spiritual Christian has accepted this great truth that righteousness is not limited because it is God's righteousness and not man's. We will never be more righteous than we were the moment we were born again. Righteousness does not depend upon works. However, we do grow in the knowledge of what righteousness means and how it affects our lives. We begin to see ourselves as God sees us—free from the past. All sin is removed, along with the guilt and condemnation.

Beloved, now are we the sons of God...

1 John 3:2

We look and talk like a child of God. We're not sad, depressed, or defeated. Instead, we smile and our shoulders are held high. We walk the victory walk; we talk the victory talk. Our prayers are answered because we come to Him with boldness and confidence. We know we are worthy because of what Jesus did at Calvary.

We no longer confess, "I am an old sinner saved by grace." But rather we can say, "I was a sinner, but now I am saved and set free from my past by the grace of God!" We have the freedom, ability, confidence and boldness to enter into the throne room of God and fellowship with Him.

Let us therefore come boldly into the throne of grace, that we may obtain mercy, and find grace to help in time of need.

Hebrews 4:16

Peace and joy in the Holy Ghost

The spiritual Christian understands righteousness—that it places us in right standing with God. Serving God is more than just going to heaven after physical death. Please don't misunderstand—I don't want to play down going to heaven or its importance. Going to heaven is a very good reason for serving God, but it should not be the *only* reason for serving Him.

I believe in heaven and look forward with great anticipation to that great day when I get to go! Life is pretty much a bum ride because of Adam's sin in the garden. It is because of Jesus' death on the cross at Calvary that it is worth living. The spiritual Christian has this revelation and gets more out of serving God. It's as though we have an insurance policy guaranteeing us passage to heaven when we die. In addition, we know that faithfully serving God here on earth will bring even greater joy when we arrive there.

> **For the kingdom of God is not meat and drink; but righteousness, and peace, and joy in the Holy Ghost.**
> **Romans 14:17**

For the spiritual Christian, walking and living the Christian life by faith is not a struggle. It is peace and joy in the Holy Ghost. It is not difficult to serve God when we let Him become *Lord* of our lives. Every day is a victory! We have the hope of heaven and look forward to being reunited with our loved ones and in the presence of Jesus forever. Knowing that we will never be separated from our loved ones is such a glorious thought. Right now, though, it's a joy to know the Lord is my Shepherd and that I have no want or lack. It's a joy to know the Lord directs my path daily to still waters and to safety. To know His presence is with me, anointing me, and that He will give me goodness and mercy now.

More than a conqueror

The Christian life is not merely waiting and existing until the coming of the Lord. A believer walking in power and confidence is an example to the unbeliever. The believer is an imitator of Christ.

> **Therefore be imitators of God—copy Him and follow His example—as well-beloved children [imitate their father].**
> **Ephesians 5:1 (AMP)**

We are to walk the walk that Jesus commanded us to walk. We are to take every opportunity to boldly declare Jesus to our generation. We are to be witnesses for Christ wherever we may be—in our neighborhood, community, place of business, riding the bus or talking on the phone. The power of Christ is revealed through spiritual Christians to the lost and hurting.

> **But you shall receive power—ability, efficiency and might—when the Holy Spirit has come upon you; and you shall be My witnesses in Jerusalem and all Judea and Samaria and to the ends—the very bounds of the earth.**
>
> **Acts 1:8 (AMP)**

Spiritual believers have no fear. We are not intimidated by people because we have God's ability at work in us. God's might and power are within us to witness and take control of inferiority and fear.

> **Now we have not received the spirit (that belongs to) the world, but the (Holy) Spirit Who is from God, [given to us] that we might realize and comprehend and appreciate the gifts (of divine favor and blessing so freely and lavishly) bestowed on us by God.**
>
> **1 Corinthians 2:12 (AMP)**

When we are spiritual rather than carnal, it means we are no longer of the world—we are of God. Our desires are the desires of the Holy Spirit. To be conquerors in this world! Not to just barely get by, but to *win* and bring many other people into the kingdom of God in the process.

> **Nay, in all these things we are more than conquerors through him that loved us. For I am persuaded, that neither death, nor life, nor angels, nor principalities, nor powers, not things present, nor things to come, Nor height, nor depth, nor any other creature, shall be able**

to separate us from the love of God, which is in Christ
Jesus our Lord.

Romans 8:37-39

Mark 16:17 and 18 contain a commandment given to us by Jesus. As
spiritual believers, we obey this command and cast out devils and lay hands
on the sick. Signs and wonders follow us. We are conquerors in all
circumstances; with patience we run the course that is set before us.

The Five Ministry Gifts

And His gifts were [varied; He Himself appointed and
gave men to us,] some to be apostles (special
messengers), some prophets (inspired preachers and
expounders), some evangelists (preachers of the Gospel,
traveling missionaries), some pastors (shepherds of His
flock) and teachers.

His intention was the perfecting and full equipping
of the saints (His consecrated people). [that they should
do] the work of ministering toward building up Christ's
body (the church),

[That it might develop] until we all attain oneness in
the faith and in the comprehension of the full and accurate
knowledge of the Son of God; that [we might arrive] at
really mature manhood—the completeness of personality
which is nothing less than the standard height of Christ's
own perfection—the measure of the stature of the fullness
of the Christ, and the completeness found in Him.

So then, we may no longer be children, tossed [like
ships] to and fro between chance gusts of teaching, and
wavering with every changing wind of doctrine, [the prey
of] the cunning and cleverness of unscrupulous men,
(gamblers engaged) in every shifting form of trickery in
inventing errors to mislead.

Rather, let our lives lovingly express truth in all things—speaking truly, dealing truly, living truly. Enfolded in love, let us grow up in every way and in all things into Him, Who is the Head [even] Christ, the Messiah, the Anointed One.

For because of Him the whole body (the church in all its various parts closely) joined and firmly knit together by the joints and ligaments with which it is supplied, when each part [with power adapted to its need] is working properly (in all its functions), grows to full maturity, building itself up in love.

Ephesians 4:11-16 (AMP)

The church needs the five ministries: the apostle, prophet, evangelist, pastor, and teacher. God gave these ministry gifts to the body of Christ to teach the uncompromised truth so the Church will develop to full maturity. As we mature through the instruction that we receive, we will do more than come to church. We will do the work of the ministry, building up the other members of the body of Christ.

All five of the ministries are needed. They are all important to bring about the maturity needed. It takes all five to give Christians a proper balance. We cannot be under the teaching of just one of the special gifts. If we accept only one, we will never be able to develop fully.

When the five ministries and their teaching are received, the Christian grows out of the childhood stages and matures as he applies the Word of God to his life. The result is love for and the desire to help other members of the body of Christ. Competition is eliminated because everyone works toward the common goal of bringing the entire world to the knowledge of the truth that Jesus Christ is Lord.

Because of our strong foundations, we no longer chase after, or are fooled by, false doctrines. When something is done or taught and we do not bear witness with it, we do not fall or become confused. Instead, we stand on the apostles' doctrine with Jesus Christ being the chief cornerstone (Ephesians 2:20).

Every mature Christian accepts the gift of the pastor. The pastor loves, guides and gives to the flock. He feeds them and protects them and watches for wolves. He shares his pulpit with the other four ministry gifts, making sure that his flock receives a balanced diet of the Word of God. If you don't have a pastor like this, you should find one. Balanced teaching through all the gifts is essential to spiritual growth.

These first few chapters have given brief yet concise descriptions of the natural man, the carnal man and the spiritual man—who they are and what they do. It is my intention in the following chapters to show how believers can develop spiritual maturity.

Chapter 4
Renew Your Mind

I beseech you therefore, brethren, by the mercies of God, that ye present your bodies a living sacrifice, holy, acceptable unto God, which is your reasonable service. And be not conformed to this world: but be ye transformed by the renewing of your mind, that ye may prove what is that good, and acceptable, and perfect, will of God.

Romans 12:1,2

Notice Paul said, "I beseech you therefore, *brethren*." This lets us know that he was talking to the Christians. After we have exercised our will to accept Jesus and become born again, we have a further responsibility. That responsibility is to give all that we are to God. He said not to be tied to or entangled with the world, but to be renewed in our thinking.

Man is a triune being

First Thessalonians 5:23 says that man is a spirit, he has a soul and he lives in a body. After the new birth the life of God dwells in the spirit of man. The change in the spirit is instantaneous. The reign of death under the rule of Satan is transformed into the vibrant life of God. Through the wooing of the Holy Spirit, the mind gains the capacity to change and accept Jesus. The spirit does not have this capability.

The soul of man is composed of the mind, will and emotions. The change that takes place in the soul is a gradual and progressive one. The soul is so closely associated with the spirit that we cannot always tell where one ends and the other begins. The only sure way to differentiate between the spirit and the soul is through the Word of God.

For the word of God is quick, and powerful, and sharper than any two-edged sword, piercing even to the dividing asunder of the soul and spirit...

Hebrews 4:12

The Word of God is alive, powerful, and able to separate the two. The spirit and the soul work together. It takes the constant transformation of the mind through the Word of God to draw out and utilize the fullness of God within man's spirit. If after being born again, we do not put something into our minds concerning the new life within, it will revert back to the way it was prior to the new birth. The patterns of the old man will regain the ascendancy because the mind has nothing except prior experiences with which to make judgments and decisions.

We humans live in a body. Our bodies are our "earth suits." The body is not the real person—it is only the *residence* of the real person. The body functions through the five senses: seeing, hearing, tasting, smelling, and feeling. As has been mentioned before, the person who is not born again is not alive unto God and is controlled by those five senses. The body's function is to house the born-again spirit and soul. At death, the spirit and soul depart from the earthly body. The body, having fulfilled its purpose, begins to decay.

The born-again Christian is a triune being. The spirit, soul and body must function together to have an effect. One part of that trinity is ineffective without the other. The born-again spirit, if left untapped, is useless. The unrenewed mind cannot draw from the limitless potential of God's life within the spirit. Neither the spirit nor the soul can have any effect unless channeled through the body. They must all function together to fulfill God's ultimate intention for the believer.

The spirit of man

11 For what man knoweth the things of a man, save the spirit of man which is in him? even so the things of God knoweth no man, but the Spirit of God. 12 Now we have received, not the spirit of the world, but the spirit which is of God; that we might know the things that are freely given to us of God.

1 Corinthians 2:11-12 (KJV)

When we are born again, we receive Him into our spirits. Paul said that we have not received the spirit of the world but the Spirit of God that we might know the things that are freely given of God.

And you *hath he quickened*, who were dead in trespasses and sins...

Ephesians 2:1 (KJV)

When God's Spirit is united with man's spirit, the believer is made alive unto God. We receive God's very nature within us—the nature that knows no bounds. The Bible says that the kingdom of God is within each believer (Luke 17:21). It also states in Romans 14:17 that the kingdom of God is righteousness, peace, and joy in the Holy Ghost. The word *kingdom* in these verses, is translated from the Greek word, *basileia*, which means *reign* (a foundation of power). As born-again Christians, we have received power to rule and reign over Satan in our spirits. Our spirits can be foundations of power here on earth!

And ye are complete in him, which is the head of all principality and power...

Colossians 2:10 (KJV)

This scripture tells us that we are complete in Christ. This is the same principle we discussed in the introduction. When a baby is born, all the internal organs are there but they must develop fully to attain maximum capacity. We must also learn how to develop toward maturity in the soul or thinking realm. The believer can learn to let the spirit be the king, let the soul be the servant and let the body be the slave. Our spirits, however, cannot rule until our minds have been developed and renewed to the things of God.

The soul of man

The soul has much to do with the Christian walk. There are differing opinions about spiritual growth. Some say that it occurs in the spirit of man, but I believe and teach that the real development takes place in the area of the soul. The goal is for our will to become God's will, for our mind to become God's mind and for our emotions to respond as God would.

The soul can only become a servant to the spirit as it develops, surrenders, submits or commits to the spirit. The will decides which is in control—our spirits or our emotions. Many Christians are controlled by their emotions because they have never learned how to control them. Some have been taught, but have chosen to live a defeated life rather than a victorious one.

> **Ever learning, and never able to come to the knowledge of the truth.**
>
> **2 Timothy 3:7 (KJV)**

It is difficult for me to understand how people who know the truth will not do what they know to do to be an overcomer. I have not overcome obstacles because I am a pastor. I am victorious because I am an heir of God and a joint-heir with Jesus. I want to be happy, so when obstacles come I think the thoughts of God and I talk the talk of God. Many times in my life I have had the opportunity to be down, discouraged and to feel sorry for myself, but I chose to let the Spirit of God control instead of my emotions. Looking at and talking about the circumstances can make us feel sad and depressed, but looking at God's Word and talking God's Word will change our feelings.

Controlling thoughts

8 Finally, brethren, whatsoever things are true, whatsoever things *are* honest, whatsoever things *are* just, whatsoever things *are* pure, whatsoever things *are* lovely, whatsoever things *are* of good report; if *there be* any virtue, and if *there be* any praise, think on these things. 9 Those things, which ye have both learned, and received, and heard, and seen in me, do: and the God of peace shall be with you.

Philippians 4:8-9 (KJV)

The child of God must take control of his thoughts. Paul said to think thoughts that are good. Why? Because God is good.

Every good gift and every perfect gift is from above, and cometh down from the Father of lights, with whom is no variableness, neither shadow of turning.

James 1:17 (KJV)

When we think of things that are pure, lovely, and of good report, we allow the virtue that is in our spirits to flow freely in our minds. Paul told those around him to do the things that they heard and saw in him. He was saying that they had seen him face opposition, pain and many other problems, but they saw that he always thought the thoughts of God and took positive steps. He praised God instead of giving in to his feelings!

One good example is the time Paul and Silas were put in jail after having been beaten for preaching the gospel. They did not sit around and have a "pity party," making all kinds of negative statements such as, "I wonder why God let this happen to us when we've been casting out devils, healing the sick, preaching the gospel?". No! They did the opposite! They sang praises at midnight, an earthquake came and the prison doors flew open. The result of these praises was their freedom and, even better, the jailer received Jesus as Savior (Acts 16:25-31). They chose to think on the good things rather than the bad and God moved for them. Right now, take control of your thoughts. Think good thoughts—don't let Satan destroy your day.

> **This *is* the day *which* the LORD hath made; we will rejoice and be glad in it.**
>
> **Psalms 118:24 (KJV)**

You can choose the thoughts you think. You have a will—this gives you the right to make choices. You are a servant to the one you choose to give your will to. Thoughts can decide our feelings. What we think on becomes our reality.

> **Know ye not, that to whom ye yield yourselves servants to obey, his servants ye are to whom ye obey...**
>
> **Romans 6:16 (KJV)**

Whatever we do with the thoughts that enter our minds will determine how we live our lives. Every thought must be dealt with individually. One can come from what is stored in the mind or from outside circumstances—be it from God or Satan.

> **(For the weapons of our warfare *are* not carnal, but mighty through God to the pulling down of strong holds;) 5 Casting down imaginations, and every high thing that exalteth itself against the knowledge of God, and bringing**

into captivity every thought to the obedience of Christ…
2 Corinthians 10:4,5 (KJV)

There are three words that I would like to point out in these two verses of scripture: *thoughts, imaginations,* and *strongholds*. A thought, whether it be from God or the devil, will turn into an imagination if held onto. It then progresses into a stronghold. If the thought, imagination and stronghold are from God, then nothing from Satan can interfere. We can be victorious because our minds are locked into our spirits. Our bodies will then follow through. The body will obey what is being sent through the mind, and the spirit controls the mind.

If the thought is from the devil or is a negative thought, the solution is to cast it down with prayer or by singing praises unto God. Don't let that evil or bad thought turn into an imagination (fear, worry or unbelief). If it does, you are headed for the next step—a stronghold. Satan then has you thinking what he wants you to think, and the result is a defeated life.

Just because Satan puts evil thoughts in our minds does not mean we have sinned. It becomes sin when we refuse to deal with the thoughts and allow them to develop. When we dwell on certain thoughts they change ownership and we become obedient to them. Satan cannot read our minds. This may come as a surprise to some, but it is true. He may give a thought, but we have the opportunity to reject or entertain it. He does not know what we are thinking until we speak about it or act on it.

1 If ye then be risen with Christ, seek those things
which are above, where Christ sitteth on the right hand
of God. 2 Set your affection on things above, not on things
on the earth. 3 For ye are dead, and your life is hid with
Christ in God.
Colossians 3:1-3 (KJV)

Paul said to think and seek the things of God, not the things of the world. Don't sit around and worry. Your old life is gone. You now have the life of God and are hidden in Christ when you are obedient to Him. Realize that Satan does not know everything. If he knew everything, he would have known exactly where Jesus was and who He was at birth. He would not have killed all the babies in Bethlehem who were two years and under (Matthew 2:16). Jesus would not have been crucified either.

Which none of the princes of this world knew: for had they known *it*, they would not have crucified the Lord of glory. 1 Corinthians 2:8 (KJV)

The more we renew our minds to the things of God, the more we think like God. We are able to recognize where every thought comes from.

The body

19 What? know ye not that your body is the temple of the Holy Ghost *which is* in you, which ye have of God, and ye are not your own? 20 For ye are bought with a price: therefore glorify God in your body, and in your spirit, which are God's.

1 Corinthians 6:19,20 (KJV)

When we are born again God chooses to dwell in our bodies here on the earth. As our minds are renewed to the Lord, our bodies need no longer control us. Before the new birth man is controlled by his senses— what he tastes, smells, hears, sees and feels. As the believer meditates and renews his or her thinking, new information is stored in the mind. When, at the same time, the body sends a message of, say, a disease symptom to the brain, the believer will exercise self-control which has been developed by the Spirit of God. Then, instead of allowing the body to rule, the believer will rule his body.

On Sunday morning your body may tell you to stay home from church and have "bedside assembly."

"It's all right," your body says. "You need the rest." Or…"You don't need to pray an hour every day." You may make the commitment to pray but when you begin your body will try to sleep. Make it obey you.

When you start meditating in the Word your body will again try to rule you. You have God's power. Direct your mind to thinking the thoughts of God. By renewing the mind every day you are able to hear the voice of your spirit. When you make the decision to follow that voice of the spirit, your body will follow suit.

I have said earlier that while you are under the direction of your bodily desires, your spirit is unable to make the decision. When your will becomes the will of the Spirit, then your spirit takes control. The spirit becomes king, your soul becomes the servant, and your body becomes a slave to your soul.

Don't let the body be king. Exercise temperance (self-control). When you give in to your body you are unable to accomplish God's desire for your life. If you are falling short in the area of appetite, make the quality decision to push that plate back! Going on a diet is not the answer. Self-control is the answer. Do everything you do with moderation at all times.

I have found that I must discipline myself each day, not just when I feel like it. I hardly ever "feel" like it! I am like most people—I love to eat. I eat to live, though, rather than live to eat. I watch what I put in my mouth, as well as the time that it goes in. I do eat some sweets, but only in moderation. The secret is moderation.

Millions of dollars are spent on diets or aids for weight loss every year. Those who partake may lose weight rapidly, but the problem lies in keeping that weight off and preventing more from coming back. This is why I personally don't believe in dieting. I believe self-control is the answer.

If you are overweight, decide what you are going to do about it—then do it! But make sure it's not an "overnight remedy." Take responsibility for bringing your body under control.

I have a good friend who had been overweight for several years. He is a professional person and knew that his weight was a hindrance to both his job and his testimony for Christ. Deciding to do something about it, he lost ninety pounds over a period of fourteen months. He knew if he tried to lose it in two or three months, it would not last. He began to exercise self-control. He ate less than usual each time he sat down to a meal and watched the kinds of food that he ate. He is proud of his accomplishment because he did not let his flesh win!

My reference to anyone with a weight problem is not meant to condemn. It is, however, important for each believer to make the quality decision to be spirit-controlled. And to be spirit-controlled, we must have self-control.

If you smoke cigarettes, you realize it is not good for your health. It is destroying your body. Surely you are not going to let that little white and brown "coffin nail" rule you. When your mind begins rationalizing the need for one, take the scriptures, memorize, and confess them. Pray in the spirit, sing praises, and call a prayer partner to agree with you in prayer. God has given you power over all things to be able to rule and reign in this life.

For if by one man's offence death reigned by one; much more they which receive abundance of grace and of the gift of righteousness shall reign in life by one, Jesus Christ.

Romans 5:17 (KJV)

God has given believers the power to be victorious every day, but we are the only ones who can exercise this authority. I have used overeating and smoking as only two of the areas in which self-control is needed. There are many others, but in my experience these seem to be the most common ones.

Growing into maturity by renewing our minds is perpetual. There is no such thing as staying in one place. We either progress or regress. Paul said, **"But this one thing I do, forgetting those things which are behind, and reaching forth unto those things which are before, I press toward the mark for the prize of the high calling of God in Christ Jesus."** **Philippians 3:13 AP**

Every day I have a goal—something I want to achieve. I know I must press and push forward to obtain it. A winner never quits and a quitter never wins. Obstacles are there, but I am a winner! You can be too!

Chapter 5
The Power of Words

Death and life *are* in the power of the tongue: and they that love it shall eat the fruit thereof.

Proverbs 18:21 (KJV)

The words we speak are vitally important. Words can set us free or place us in bondage. Our conversation can literally bring life or death. Most people who receive Jesus as Savior must learn how to talk in a new way. A new way is necessary because the old way, filled with negative words, produced sorrow and unhappiness.

It hurts me to hear Spirit-filled Christians talking in the negative realm. By doing so they can never actually mature or develop. We never rise above the level of our confession.

God used words to create

Just as God used words to create the heavens, the earth and man, we use the power in words to create good or bad in our lives. Words can control our future. Many things have happened in our lives, both good and bad, because of our words. We can take inventory of our lives by examining our conversation to determine if we speak and respond as Jesus would in any given situation. Do we have "weeds" or "flowers" in the gardens of our lives?

45

3 And God said, Let there be light: and there was light.

6 And God said, Let there be a firmament in the midst of the waters, and let it divide the waters from the waters.

9 And God said, Let the waters under the heaven be gathered together unto one place, and let the dry *land* appear: and it was so.

11 And God said, Let the earth bring forth grass, the herb yielding seed, *and* the fruit tree yielding fruit after his kind, whose seed *is* in itself, upon the earth: and it was so.

14 And God said, Let there be lights in the firmament of the heaven to divide the day from the night; and let them be for signs, and for seasons, and for days, and years:

20 And God said, Let the waters bring forth abundantly the moving creature that hath life, and fowl *that* may fly above the earth in the open firmament of heaven.

26 And God said, Let us make man in our image, after our likeness: and let them have dominion over the fish of the sea, and over the fowl of the air, and over the cattle, and over all the earth, and over every creeping thing that creepeth upon the earth.

Genesis 1 (KJV)

Listed above are seven scriptures in the first chapter of Genesis that declare, "God said." He actually had to speak it before it came into being. From this we understand what power there is in our words.

"...And the spirit of God moved upon the face of the waters."

Genesis 1:2 (KJV)

The Spirit was with or upon the words that God was speaking or there could have been no creation. The Spirit of God carried out what He spoke. In the same way God spoke, we speak "words" to receive the life of Christ as a new creation.

In addition to merely speaking the words, there also must be a belief in the creative power of the words we say.

9 That if thou shalt confess with thy mouth the Lord Jesus, and shalt believe in thine heart that God hath raised him from the dead, thou shalt be. 10 For with the heart man believeth unto righteousness; and with the mouth confession is made unto salvation.

Romans 10:9,10 (KJV)

Some have said that if you speak something long enough, it will happen. There is some truth to that statement, but let's clarify it.

What actually happens is that when we speak, whether by the Word of God or by Satan, we give one (God or Satan) the right to bring it to pass. Charles Capps says, "God's Word that is conceived in your heart, then formed by the tongue, and spoken out of your own mouth, becomes a spiritual force, releasing the ability of God within you." In other words, when we believe God's Word (in our hearts), then speak it forth, we will see results! Believe and then speak.

...I believed, and therefore have I spoken; we also believe, and therefore speak...

2 Corinthians 4:13 (KJV)

When we believe God's Word and it is conceived in our hearts, we have understanding. Then, as we speak, we release the force of the Holy Spirit within us to bring what has been spoken into existence.

The same thing happens in the negative realm. When we make statements that are the opposite of what God has said in His Word, we begin to believe them. Then Satan, being the god of this world, takes the words that are being spoken and causes the very things we say to come to pass. We give or deny Satan the power to do evil in our lives by the words we speak.

Keep your conversation right

Whoso offereth praise glorifieth me: and to him that ordereth *his* conversation *aright* will I shew the salvation of God.

Psalms 50:23 (KJV)

As believers we can learn to speak in agreement with the Word of God rather than what circumstances dictate. We can learn the importance of speaking what we want rather than what we don't want. When we order our conversation "aright," as the scripture says, we will see the glory of God manifested.

Paul says the conversation from the past life can be changed.

That ye put off concerning the former conversation the old man ...

Ephesians 4:22 (KJV)

Every word that Christians speak should edify both self and others. This change will not happen overnight—it takes time and diligence. But our speech is important to our growth and development as mature

Christians. We must change our thinking before we are able to change our speaking (Psalm 50:23).

> **Let no man despise thy youth; but be thou an example of the believers, in word, in conversation, in charity, in spirit, in faith, in purity.**
> **1 Timothy 4:12 (KJV)**

Paul was telling Timothy in this scripture that people watched and listened to him even in his normal conversation. Believers should be an example that reveals Christ, not only when ministering in public, but in day-to-day life.

If you are a businessperson, the way you talk with people is very important. Not only can you be a success by the words you speak, but you can also reveal Christ to others. Whether you are a secretary, laborer, teacher or businessperson, your words can be effective to those around you. Always speak positive, encouraging words—words of praise that lift up those who are listening.

> **Let the redeemed of the LORD say *so*...**
> **Psalms 107:2 (KJV)**

Idle words

> **But I say unto you, That every idle word that men shall speak, they shall give account thereof in the day of judgment.**
> **Matthew 12:36 (KJV)**

Idle words are non-productive words, lifeless words. We will each be judged by our words, both in this life and at the coming day of judgment. It is necessary for a child of God to develop the kind of vocabulary that builds a productive life.

**He that keepeth his mouth keepeth his life: *but* he
that openeth wide his lips shall have destruction.**

Proverbs13:3 (KJV)

When our words are in agreement with God's Word, those words
produce health, happiness and more. Speaking God's Word not only benefits
the speaker, but others as well. Our words will lift them up and cause
them to feel better.

**Heaviness in the heart of man maketh it stoop: but a
good word maketh it glad.**

Proverbs 12:25 (KJV)

**A soft answer turneth away wrath: but grievous words
stir up anger.**

Proverbs 15:1 (KJV)

You may not *feel* like saying good words or giving a soft answer, but
Proverbs says that a good word can make a heart glad and that a soft
answer can turn away anger. As we understand who we are in Christ, we
will want to take the responsibility of speaking positive words. Our words
reveal our level of spiritual maturity.

One person may speak evil against another person. The one who is
spoken against may be quick to retaliate with the same type of words
because he or she gives in to emotions.

It has been said, "If I respond to you in the same manner that you
have spoken to me, I have given you the power over me to make me in
your image." When a Christian responds to anger with similar anger, that
is no different from the way an unregenerated person might act. We can
change from the former man and learn to hold our peace.

Even a fool, when he holdeth his peace, is counted wise: *and* he that shutteth his lips *is esteemed* a man of understanding.

Proverbs 17:28 (KJV)

Everyone knows how difficult it is to remain quiet when we are spoken against. But the Word of God says we're wise if we keep quiet. One of the reasons why people never reach full potential in life is due to a poor attitude that is then verbalized. On the job someone will usually find negative comments to make about the company. If someone else joins in, and then another, little by little you may find yourself finding fault with the company also. Don't let yourself get caught in that trap.

Keep this policy: If you can't say positive things about the company you work for, then don't say anything at all. You won't regret it.

I've heard people say that they dread going to work. Those words only make matters worse. People may say they don't like their job, the people they work for, or the people they work with. Once again, they have let their speech cause negative things to come to them. When a person agrees to hire on with a specific business, a commitment has been made to the job. That commitment then must be walked out.

If you've been saying negative things about your job, you can change your attitude by finding the things you like about it. Begin to talk about the things you *do* like rather than what you *don't* like. Speak good words over your employer, rather than complaining about the working conditions or the pay.

Improve the conditions by having a good report to give to other employees and superiors. Soon you will be promoted and make more money because you are sowing good seeds. You should be speaking unity and production rather than division and destruction.

People with good attitudes are noticed on the job by their superiors. They are the ones who get along with others, do a satisfactory job and do not complain. They also speak positive things about their jobs.

In a case where the employee is being mistreated on the job, there are proper steps to take in correcting the situation. But complaining to other employees or siding with those who complain causes even more strife. Superiors also notice those who needlessly cause strife and division. They stand more chance of losing their job than in receiving a promotion.

Don't be a gossip

As we mature in the things of God, we will begin to speak more like a child of God than a child of darkness. Our speech will reveal Jesus Christ. There has been much harm done within the body of Christ because someone makes a mistake and then other immature or carnal Christians tell others of that mistake. Then they tell still others, and soon that person's reputation is severely damaged.

Most of the time when a person falls or makes a mistake, he or she is sorry and suffers enough for the wrong done. Why should other Christians make it worse for them? I've heard it said that the Christian army is the only one that buries its wounded. In many instances this is true.

If a brother or sister has enough confidence in you to confide a wrongdoing, then carefully consider in prayer before you ever divulge that confidence.

> **He that covereth a transgression seeketh love; but he that repeateth a matter separateth *very* friends.**
> **Proverbs 17:9 (KJV)**

When you are made aware that a sister or brother has made a mistake, talk to that person—not someone else. Go directly to God and pray. James said that the tongue is full of deadly poison. False reports have brought much harm and many wounds to good people.

A talebearer revealeth secrets: but he that is of a faithful spirit concealeth the matter.

Proverbs 11:13 (KJV)

The words of a talebearer *are* as wounds, and they go down into the innermost parts of the belly.

Proverbs18:8 (KJV)

He that goeth about *as* a talebearer revealeth secrets: therefore meddle not with him that flattereth with his lips.

Proverbs 20:19 (KJV)

20 Where no wood is, *there* the fire goeth out: so where *there is* no talebearer, the strife ceaseth. 21 *As* coals *are* to burning coals, and wood to fire; so *is* a contentious man to kindle strife. 22 The words of a talebearer *are* as wounds, and they go down into the innermost parts of the belly. 23 Burning lips and a wicked heart *are like* a potsherd covered with silver dross.

Proverbs 26:20-23 (KJV)

Many good friends have been separated by a false tongue. Talebearers have caused churches to be broken apart and split. Ministries have been deeply hurt because of those who have repeated what they've heard. We needn't be caught in Satan's snare. We can choose to speak and give only the good report. Christians are to build up and edify our brothers and sisters in Christ and avoid repeating that which is not edifying and uplifting. Our words are to be words of faith, words of life and encouragement. As we speak good over others, they will speak good over us in return!

Speak positively in bad circumstances

One of the things Sharon and I have learned to do is speak positively when the circumstances are bad. We have experienced difficult times in our lives—times that caused much pain. Often the pain was so bad we could not hold back the tears, but we chose to speak only words of life. We praised the Lord and prayed in tongues. This gave God the opportunity to bring healing and refreshment to us. It is vital to Christians to develop a life of praise.

I've heard Christians complain by saying, "I don't understand. I've done all I know to do. Why is this happening to me?" I'm not saying I've not had these same thoughts because I have. But when they came I would not let them stay in my mind. I repeatedly said, "This is the day the Lord has made. I will rejoice and be glad in it." It may take time. We must say it over and over again. In Ephesians 5:19,20 we are admonished to sing to ourselves praises and spiritual songs. Refreshment and restoration will *always* come.

If you lose your job, don't complain. Speak positive words such as, "The Lord will provide. God has something better for me. The Lord directs my path. He is my helper." Don't give in to feelings and speak negatively. Satan wants a believer to say things like, "I don't know what we're going to do," or "We'll probably lose the house, the car, the furniture and everything we have." *Don't repeat these things even though you may feel like it!*

Speak God's Word—not your feelings

In times of tests and trials we can learn to speak only positive words, words that are in agreement with God's Word. Whether newborn Christians or believers who have knowledge of these things, it's important that we do what the Word says to do whether we feel like it or not!

Our words guide and direct us. They have the power to produce life or death. Evil or negative words affect us both inwardly and outwardly. God's love within us is a vital force, and the love we give to others brings life. If we take the love within us and selfishly turn it inward, it will destroy. That is why it is so important to always speak good things.

A man's belly shall be satisfied with the fruit of his mouth; *and* with the increase of his lips shall he be filled.
Proverbs 18:20 (KJV)

It's our choice

The choice to either be fulfilled or destroyed by our words is given to each person. We can make the choice to be fulfilled by good words spoken over others and ourselves.

I remember one situation that hurt me deeply. When I was an evangelist I traveled frequently and was away from my home much of the time. I received a call late one afternoon that my daughter Tammy had been struck by an automobile and wasn't expected to live through the night.

When I arrived at the hospital and saw the extent of the injuries my daughter suffered, my emotions screamed out, "Why me, Lord? What have I done? I've been a faithful servant for years. What did I do to deserve this?" My emotions were in turmoil, but the foundation of the Word of God rose up within me and I repeated over and over again, with tears streaming down my face, "Father, I love You. I praise You. I thank You for Your love for me." I also prayed in tongues. God strengthened me inwardly through my choice of life-filled words. And my daughter was healed.

Set a correct course

Behold also the ships, which though *they be* so great, and *are* driven of fierce winds, yet are they turned about with a very small helm, whithersoever the governor listeth.
James 3:4 (KJV)

James said that the rudder of a ship is small and yet it keeps a big ship on course even in the midst of strong and fierce winds. James compared the rudder of a ship to a person's tongue. In verse 6 he says that the tongue can defile the entire body and set the course of what that person's life will be like. We can set a correct course by the words of life we speak every day.

A wholesome tongue *is* a tree of life: but perverseness therein *is* a breach in the spirit.
Proverbs 15:4 (KJV)

When we speak the right words we release God's power. But when we talk and say words contrary to God's Word, they bring bruising, hurt and brokenness in spirit. It actually grieves the heart of God when Christians fail to control their words. Most believers say bad things because they have not been taught any different. They are saying the things that they have heard all their lives, and sadly many have heard their spiritual leaders say these same things in their presence.

Don't be a stumbling block

There are those who have become stumbling blocks for people new in the walk of faith. They seem to fall into two categories. The first are those who have the intellectual knowledge of the power of the Word and want to have the respect of others by virtue of that knowledge. The second group are those who have genuinely received some revelation from the

Word concerning confession and they want everyone else to be at their level right now. A descriptive phrase has been coined for them: "confession inspectors." Both are overbearing, but for different reasons.

The first type may have heard a few messages on "what you say is what you get," but have not found out about basing every promise of God on all of the Bible, rather than a few verses and a message. Their language was as negative as anyone's before they heard about confession, yet they seem to forget that. They have a desire to correct any negative vocabulary in everyone with whom they come into contact.

This correction, however tends to bring condemnation and bondage, not freedom. They also try to make confession a law rather than seeing the grace of God. They don't see confession as the outward expression of inward faith and they are intolerant of views or beliefs contrary to what they "know."

They may speak the truth in some cases, but it is spoken without love or compassion and is comparable to the way the Pharisees spoke in Jesus' day.

The second type are those who have had a genuine change in their lives. They have truly seen the power in their words and want everyone else to have the same knowledge. They have more zeal than knowledge and are quick to correct. Many times they cause hurt and embarrassment and do more harm than good. Even though their intentions are honorable, the result is the same as those who only have the intellectual knowledge.

There is a way to correct people, but there must be a balance. The person who is speaking negatively must be made to understand why he or she is saying the wrong thing. Pointing out one's poor choice of words is not the answer. The remedy lies in gently directing that person toward the Word of God concerning the situation they are speaking negatively about.

If the person who has some knowledge of proper confession is not thoroughly grounded in what the Word says, he should say nothing. Partial truth can easily lead to confusion and error.

The person who is speaking negatively must have a teachable attitude. If that is not apparent, no revelation will come and the truth of the Word will have fallen on deaf ears. When I hear Christians speaking in the negative realm it hurts me, but I either say nothing or find a way to help them that will not hurt or embarrass. I do my utmost to speak the truth in love.

Justified or condemned

For by thy words thou shalt be justified, and by thy words thou shalt be condemned.
Matthew 12:37 (KJV)

I believe negative words can open the door for Satan to bring things to the one speaking them. Below is a list of phrases I often hear Christians say. Check to see if any of these are in your vocabulary.

I keep a cold all winter.

The kids stay sick all winter.

I get headaches all the time.

I get hay fever every spring.

My father had a heart attack—I probably will too.

My mother has high blood pressure—I'll probably have it too.

Everything I eat turns to fat.

I will probably go bald—my father did.

Every time we give extra to the work of the Lord, something always happens.

I give and never get anything back.

If I could ever get out of debt I'd pay my tithes.

If anyone gets laid off it'll be me.

I'll be in debt forever.

It looks like I'll never be able to pay all my bills.

We are always behind.

We always do without.

We will never be able to have nice things.

We don't ever get to take a vacation—we can't afford it.

We'll always be poor. We can't ever save money because something always happens.

We will never achieve our dream.

We can never build our new home.

We will always have to buy a used car. We can't afford a new one.

Come to our house and see how poor folks live.

We can't afford steak.

If anything bad is going to happen, it'll happen to me. Bad things always happen to me.

Things never go right for us/me.

Our marriage is going downhill.

Our children keep getting worse.

Every time I really start praying, something bad happens.

Nobody likes me. I'm no good to anyone.

This list of what some Christians say could go on and on. What they are doing is opening themselves up to be snared by their words.

Thou art snared with the words of thy mouth, thou art taken with the words of thy mouth.
Proverbs 6:2 (KJV)

He that keepeth his mouth keepeth his life: but he that openeth wide his lips shall have destruction.
Proverbs 13:3 (KJV)

Statements like those listed above are opposite of what God has said about His children. When we make these types of confessions, we bring snares and destruction. But if we learn to say the right words over spouse, family and self, abundant life will result. This is done by speaking what we want, rather than what we see.

Set a watch, O LORD, before my mouth; keep the door of my lips.

Psalms 141:3 (KJV)

I pray the above scripture every day because I don't want to give Satan any room to bring bad things into my life.

Neither give place to the devil.

Ephesians 4:27 (KJV)

When we open our mouths and speak according to what we see, we give place to the devil and allow his resultant authority over us.

Poor-mouth Christians

I have talked with many born-again Christians who speak negatively. There are several reasons why they speak lack into their lives. They may fear an attack by Satan if they speak the blessings of God. Or perhaps there is a false modesty used to obtain sympathy and support of others. (Traditional teaching trains Christians to do so.) Or it may be a simple case of laziness—being unwilling to learn to use the Word of God.

All of these reasons reflect a common thread of a poor self-image. Those who "poor mouth" do not look at God's righteousness but rather see nothing but filthy rags (Isaiah 64:6). The result is their eventual downfall because the negative speech will be followed by negative actions. A seed truly bears after its own kind.

Creative words

...my tongue *is* the pen of a ready writer.

Psalms 45:1 (KJV)

The words we speak should be words expressing what we want to happen rather than what we don't want to happen. Jesus is the perfect example of saying what He wanted.

Let us pass over unto the other side.
Mark 4:35 (KJV)

Jesus told His disciples to get into the boat and cross to the other side. In the process He went to sleep. Jesus meant what He said. On the way across a storm came up and the disciples became fearful. However, Jesus was not alarmed. He spoke to the storm and the waves calmed. He did not change His confession because the storm came. He rebuked the winds and the sea. He didn't say, "I don't know what we are going to do!" He spoke creatively. In the midst of bad circumstances we should speak the way we want them to be, not what they are.

God told Abraham, "I have made thee a father of many nations" (Genesis 17:4). He spoke the end result over Abraham, rather than what the situation appeared to be at the time. Abraham was past age, and Sarah's womb was dead. In the natural she could not bear a child.

God did not tell Abraham he was too old, nor did He tell Sarah her womb was dead. He said, "I have made thee a father." Abraham believed the words God spoke rather than what he and Sarah could see with their eyes. Sarah had a child because of belief in God's Word. Likewise, we can speak words of faith and confidence, rather than words of doubt and unbelief.

In 1 Samuel 17 we read how David overcame Goliath. When David saw this giant he did not think about Goliath's size. He did not compare his size to that of Goliath. Instead he compared God's size to Goliath. He did not think Goliath was too big to hit; rather, he was too big to miss! David went to Goliath speaking creative words.

45 Then said David to the Philistine, Thou comest to me with a sword, and with a spear, and with a shield: but I come to thee in the name of the LORD of hosts, the God of the armies of Israel, whom thou hast defied. 46 This day will the LORD deliver thee into mine hand; and I will smite thee, and take thine head from thee; and I will give the carcases of the host of the Philistines this day unto the fowls of the air, and to the wild beasts of the earth; that all the earth may know that there is a God in Israel. 47 And all this assembly shall know that the LORD saveth not with sword and spear: for the battle *is* the LORD'S, and he will give you into our hands.

1 Samuel 17:45-47 (KJV)

David did not let the size of the giant cause him to fear. He knew God was with him. He went toward the giant speaking words of power and destroyed the enemy. We can destroy giants in our lives as well! Keep in mind that it takes time to develop these habits. But that's what this book is all about—how to develop into a mature Christian.

Don't be discouraged

People have told me, "I tried speaking positive things and nothing happened." Or, "I spoke health to my body and got sick anyway." What is the problem here? Results do not come simply because we speak words— we must believe it! Believe first, then speak. It takes time to get the words and thoughts of God into our thinking. When we do, Satan will try us to see if we really believe what we're saying.

Since our pattern of life for years has been to walk and talk in the negative realm, we cannot expect to change overnight. This is where many people fail. They start out right, but become discouraged when everything they speak does not immediately come to pass.

If you fail in an area or get sick as you try to apply the Word of God, so what? As a child you stumbled and fell, but you always got back up and walked again. In school when you took a test and failed, or when you failed a grade, you repeated it until you passed. The same principle applies in confessing God's Word. When something goes wrong, get up and start again until you win. The circumstances only get worse if you give up.

> **Rejoice not against me, O mine enemy: when I fall, I shall arise; when I sit in darkness, the LORD *shall be* a light unto me.**
>
> **Micah 7:8 (KJV)**

Several years ago a friend gave me an immature peach tree. He said, "Don, when the tree blooms pinch off the buds."

"Why should I pinch off the buds? I want peaches."

He replied, "If you leave them on, it will produce peaches the first year. When that happens all the tree's energy is given to producing peaches and the tree will be weak." He continued to explain that if I pinched off the buds the first year and allowed the tree to grow strong roots and branches, I would always have good peaches. That made a lot of sense to me.

We can do the same. We can speak God's Word, and yet give ourselves time to lay a strong foundation before trying to operate at the same level of someone who has been walking in the Word for several years. It's important for a believer to speak according to his or her own faith level. Take one step at a time, one day at a time. As it takes time to learn and develop in the natural realm, it is the same in the kingdom of God.

> **...the words that I speak unto you, *they* are spirit, and *they* are life.**
>
> **John 6:63 (KJV)**

As we mature we will begin to speak by the Spirit. When our words are Spirit and life, as Jesus' words were, we will see results. We cannot speak out of emotion, greed, or selfishness and expect circumstances to change. When our desires become God's desires and our lives become God's life, the results will be God's results.

Don't pray the problem

Therefore I say unto you, What things soever ye desire, when ye pray, believe that ye receive *them*, and ye shall have *them*.

Mark 11:24 (KJV)

Many people fail to get answers from God because they go to Him and tell Him how bad the situation is, rather than telling Him what they want done about the situation. Some women who have unsaved husbands are continually telling God and everyone else how bad their husbands are.

If you have an unsaved spouse, tell God what you want that spouse to be instead of what the person is now. Praying the problem has no effect. An effective prayer is to tell God what we desire the situation to be like.

Jesus is our intercessor, and when we pray to God in Jesus' name, we can only pray the things that He can present to the Father. Since He can present only positive prayers to the Father, your petition must be positive.

...consider the Apostle and High Priest of our profession, Christ Jesus...

Hebrews 3:1 (KJV)

When Jesus was here on earth, He was sent from God to be an apostle to all men. He finished that work and is now at the right hand of the Father ever living to make intercession for believers. He keeps our confession before the Father as long as it is a confession of faith.

> ...**seeing he ever liveth to make intercession for them.**
> **Hebrews 7:25 (KJV)**

> **For Christ is not entered into the holy places made with hands, *which are* the figures of the true; but into heaven itself, now to appear in the presence of God for us...**
> **Hebrews 9:24 (KJV)**

Don't get under bondage

In my travels around the country as a speaker in seminars and camp meetings I have met people who need prayer or need someone to pray the prayer of agreement with them. They have definite needs but are afraid to tell anyone what the situation is because they fear a rebuke if a "bad confession" is made. This is a sad commentary for the walk of love. If there is a need for a prayer of agreement, the need must be expressed. Otherwise, how can that prayer partner agree?

The word *agree* means to be absolutely harmonious as an orchestra would be in complete harmony. The person with whom you are in agreement must care enough to make your situation a priority over what is going on in his or her life at the time. You can't be in agreement until both of you have an understanding. This does not mean to go around continually speaking about all our problems, but rather to speak it to the one who will agree in prayer.

Two kinds of truth

I've heard people say, "I'm not going to say that I'm healed when I know that I'm sick."

I, in turn, ask the question, "Why not?"

This person has not matured to the point of understanding that there are two kinds of truth.

1) There is *physical truth*. This is what is discerned with the five senses. It may be financial problems, unemployment, disease, or family problems. If you are sick you are sick, but the good news is, you don't have to stay in that condition. There is something better.

2) There is *revelation truth*. This is what God's Word says about you and the situations that you are presently in.

Who his own self bare our sins in his own body on the tree, that we, being dead to sins, should live unto righteousness: by whose stripes ye were healed.

1 Peter 2:24 (KJV)

Notice that the healing in the above scripture is a past action. It is not going to happen in the future. When we say we believe God is *going* to heal, we are putting it in the future. The Word says He has *already* done it! At Calvary He provided healing for all believers. As we renew our minds through the Word of God, we obtain revelation truth and can say with absolute surety, "I believe that I am healed by the stripes of Jesus."

That revelation truth taps into the life and light of God within our spirits and consumes the darkness of sickness or disease. It does not mean speaking a lie. It means changing the natural by the supernatural.

While we look not at the things which are seen, but at the things which are not seen: for the things which are seen *are* temporal; but the things which are not seen *are* eternal.

2 Corinthians 4:18 (KJV)

The spirit world is infinitely more powerful than the natural world. The things that are seen and felt are subject to change.

For I *am* the LORD, I change not…
Malachi 3:6 (KJV)

The power of God is greater than any circumstance. Believe God's Word. Speak Scripture rather than what you see or feel.

…let the weak say, I *am* strong.
Joel 3:10 (KJV)

It's not a lie to speak and say what God says. Previously I gave a number of statements that people say in the negative realm. When they are making those statements it may be that nothing has yet happened, but their belief and consequent confession will bring the unseen into existence. Is that telling a lie?

And base things of the world, and things which are despised, hath God chosen, *yea*, and things which are not, to bring to nought things that are…
1 Corinthians 1:28 (KJV)

Paul said the situations that we face are changed and brought to nought by the Spirit of God. The things that "are not" change what "is." Instead of believing and speaking the negative, believe and speak God's blessings over the situations.

A young man in my church recently called and said, "Pastor, I want to give you a good report. I have been unemployed for several weeks, but my wife and I have been speaking a good job, a particular job that I wanted.

"The hope in getting this job was nearly impossible because the company had laid off people. I was told there were 6,000 people who wanted the job. This fact also tried to discourage us, but I disregarded all the negative. My wife and I spoke and agreed for that job and were not moved by the circumstances. They called me up at 3:30 in the morning and told me to come to work."

This young man did not tell a lie. The things that "were not" changed the things that "were." Remember, don't keep calling the things that "are" as though they "are." Call them as you want them to be.

Once a person was doing some volunteer work in one of my offices. Each time I went into the room where she was working, she said, "I don't have a runny nose."

I asked, "Why do you keep wiping it then?"

She was telling a lie—she did have a runny nose. She didn't understand the true meaning of confession. I began to share the Word with her and then had her confess, "I believe that I receive my healing into my body by the stripes of Jesus." Healing had already been provided for her, but it was up to her to believe and receive healing into her body.

The words we speak can be words of life instead of words of death. We've all heard people say, "That just tickled me to death." Of course, that's only a figure of speech, but why give Satan any room? It would sound better to say, "That tickled me to life."

"That scared me to death," is another common saying. If you are frightened by a situation, adding to it by negative words can do nothing but harm. Put life into your vocabulary. Words work for us or against us—we have the choice.

Fight the good fight of faith, lay hold on eternal life, whereunto thou art also called, and hast professed a good profession before many witnesses.
1 Timothy 6:12 (KJV)

Chapter 6
Forgiveness

25 And when ye stand praying, forgive, if ye have ought against any: that your Father also which is in heaven may forgive you your trespasses. 26 But if ye do not forgive, neither will your Father which is in heaven forgive your trespasses.

Mark 11:25,26 (KJV)

Learning to forgive is another vital step toward spiritual growth. A Christian who is holding on to unforgiveness cannot fully develop. God cannot forgive those who cling to unforgiveness because unforgiveness is a present sin, not a past one.

Many people ask God to give them the desires in their heart as instructed in Mark 11:24, yet ignore the prerequisite of verses 25 and 26. We must forgive those who have offended us, hurt us or spoken against us. We must loose or release them from any sin they have committed against us. Notice that He said to forgive when we pray. He did not tell us to pray for God to forgive them—He said we are to forgive them!

Go to your brother

Many people miss it by saying, "I didn't do anything to him. He's the one who treated me badly. Let him come to me and I will forgive him." This is not what the Bible says to do.

15 Moreover if thy brother shall trespass against thee, go and tell him his fault between thee and him alone: if he shall hear thee, thou hast gained thy brother. 16 But if he will not hear *thee, then* take with thee one or two more, that in the mouth of two or three witnesses every word may be established. 17 And if he shall neglect to hear them, tell *it* unto the church: but if he neglect to hear the church, let him be unto thee as an heathen man and a publican.

Matthew 18:15-17 (KJV)

If my brother in Christ speaks against me and hurts me, I'm to go to him first—not to someone else in the church. I am to go to him and make the effort to resolve the issue and forgive him. If he hears me I've regained him as a brother. If not, I'm instructed to go back to him with one or two more believers so that in the mouth of two or three witnesses every word will be established. If he still will not hear, then I am to take it to the church. If he neglects to hear the church, then I am to let him be to me as a heathen. He need not be a thorn in my side. This is how scripture clearly instructs us to handle such matters.

How many times should I forgive him?

21 Then came Peter to him, and said, Lord, how oft shall my brother sin against me, and I forgive him? till seven times? 22 Jesus saith unto him, I say not unto thee, Until seven times: but, Until seventy times seven.

Matthew 18:21,22 (KJV)

In these two verses of scripture Jesus is showing the responsibility of Christians. He is not saying to forgive 490 times in one day, but that *the power we have to forgive is unlimited*! No matter what a person does against us, we have the power to keep forgiving! We need not hold a grudge or hard feelings against this person. Jesus has forgiven us, and we in turn have the freedom to forgive others.

Release them and you'll be released

...Whatsoever ye shall bind on earth shall be bound in heaven: and whatsoever ye shall loose on earth shall be loosed in heaven.

Matthew 18:18 (KJV)

Jesus is saying here that what we do not forgive on earth is not forgiven in heaven. Jesus forgave us of all our sins; likewise, we are to forgive anyone who hurts us. If we don't forgive, the very sin we retain will come back on us!

Many times we see situations where the son of an alcoholic father will say, "I will never be like my father." Time passes on, and he becomes an alcoholic. Why? Because he will not forgive his father. The same thing is true with people who have been abused by their parents. They often turn out to be child abusers because they won't forgive the one who abused them. The truth is, when we hold on to unforgiveness, we're hurting ourselves. Life is so short—turn loose, forgive and live free.

If you don't forgive you'll be tormented

Jesus speaks more about forgiveness in Matthew 18:23-25. He told of a man who owed a large sum of money. The king demanded that the debt be paid in full. If he could not pay, his wife, his children and all his possessions would be sold to pay the debt. The servant fell down and cried for mercy before the king. The king had compassion on him and forgave him. He was freed from the debt by the king!

The servant then left the king and went to a man who owed him a debt. In comparison to what he had owed the king, the amount was very small. The servant took the man who was in debt to him by the throat and told him to pay all that he owed. The debtor fell down at his feet and begged, "Have patience with me, and I will pay you all I owe you." The servant would not wait. He had the debtor thrown in jail until the debt was paid in full.

Soon the king learned what the servant had done. The king called the servant whom he had forgiven to him and said, "You evil-hearted wretch! Here I forgave you of all that tremendous debt, just because you asked me to. Shouldn't you have mercy on others, just as I had mercy on you?" (TLB) The king then turned the servant over to the "tormentors" until he paid all that was owed.

> **So likewise shall my heavenly Father do also unto you, if ye from your hearts forgive not every one his brother their trespasses.**
> **Matthew 18:35 (KJV)**

Jesus said if we do not forgive others for what they have done, we will be turned over to the tormentors. The person with an unforgiving attitude has a life full of confusion, strife and bitterness and will be subject to the torment of Satan until there is a heart to forgive.

Bitterness

> **31 Let all bitterness, and wrath, and anger, and clamour, and evil speaking, be put away from you, with all malice: 32 And be ye kind one to another, tenderhearted, forgiving one another, even as God for Christ's sake hath forgiven you.**
> **Ephesians 4:31,32 (KJV)**

When there is no forgiveness, bitterness takes root in the heart. A person driven by bitterness speaks words of bitterness. King Saul was consumed with bitterness. Due to his acts of disobedience, he lost his anointing to be king of Israel. The anointing was transferred to young David. Saul's bitter feelings controlled him because he would not forgive David, even though David had done no harm to him.

Saul and his army chased David throughout the land trying to kill him. When David killed Goliath, the people of Israel praised David's act and it infuriated Saul even more. Because he chose not to forgive, Saul's remaining days on earth were spent in unhappiness, strife and inner torment.

The same thing happens today when people in ministry become jealous of one another. Bitterness creeps in and Christians are set at odds against each other. As a result, the work of the Lord is hindered, much to Satan's delight. What difference does it really make whom God uses as long as His will is accomplished?

A root of bitterness is like an infected sore. Until it is dealt with the situation continually gets worse. The one who refuses to forgive is the one who suffers. When a person is filled with the effects of bitterness, God cannot help. If there is something you're holding on to and haven't forgiven, it will fester like a sore. It cannot be covered up. *Take the steps now to get rid of it*—no matter who the person is or what wrong has been done. We hurt only ourselves and make our lives miserable through bitterness.

Forgive by faith

You may feel that it's impossible for you to forgive, but that's not true. There was a godly woman who lived in the western part of the United States. She had a daughter who attended a Bible college and worked part time. As the daughter was returning home from her job one evening, she was raped and stabbed to death and her body thrown by the side of the road.

This mother was a widow—her daughter was all she had. With her daughter gone, she felt as if she had nothing. As time passed she began to fill the void inside her with hatred because of bitterness toward the unknown murderer. She wondered why God had let this happen to her, especially since her daughter was studying to be a missionary. Her friends could no longer enjoy her company because of her attitude.

Finally the murderer was caught and pleaded guilty to the crime. She began to hate even more because she now knew who the man was. She thought to herself over and over, "Why should he live when my daughter is dead?" Two years passed and she was miserable. The bitterness within tormented her day and night to the point that she pushed her friends away. Eventually she had no friends and was all alone.

One day as she sat in a Sunday school class, a lesson on love and forgiveness pierced that barrier she had built around herself. These words began to well up inside her: "Set yourself free from your prison of hate. Forgive, and you will be free." She was so bound by bitterness that she did not know how to begin. Someone told her of Matthew 6:14 that says, "For if ye forgive men their trespasses, your heavenly Father will also forgive you." By faith she made the effort.

She purchased several Bibles and sent them to the penitentiary where the murderer was serving his life sentence. She asked that one be delivered personally to the man who had murdered her daughter. She sent this message with it: "I forgive you. Jesus said, 'Love one another as I have loved you.'" Then she signed her name. As she did so, it was as if a great weight was lifted from her. *She was free!* She found peace at last because she forgave him. She also prayed for him to receive Jesus as his Savior.

Several months passed. One day a phone call came from a friend. "I have a letter to share with you," she said. "It's from the man in prison to whom you sent a Bible, the man who killed your daughter." The man explained in the letter that he had accepted Jesus as his Savior because of the Bible and the message that was sent with it. He went on to say that he had never been given a gift before, and because she showed him such forgiveness, he was able to believe that God would do the same for him.

His life was totally changed. He now conducts Bible studies in the prison. Other inmates have been saved because of his testimony and witness. The woman continues to support him with financial aid and prayer. He has become the missionary that her daughter had planned to be. When she released him by forgiving him, freedom came to her. Once again, life was worth living.

You may have been hurt emotionally by your spouse, treated wrong, cheated, lied about or stripped of everything. No matter what has happened, turn loose of bitterness now. You are the one who will be consumed by it—not the other person.

Forgive and forget

In the beginning of this chapter I stated that as believers we are unable to grow until we learn to forgive. Now perhaps it is more apparent how unforgiveness of past hurts can hinder and keep us from loving and trusting other people.

If you have divorced and remarried and have not forgiven your former spouse, you will never be able to have the kind of marriage you could have if you would turn loose and set yourself free.

A woman may learn that her husband has been unfaithful to her. She decides to stay in the marriage and tells him that she has forgiven him. She continues to be a dutiful wife, but makes life hell on earth for him because she is cold and flaunts her moral "superiority."

She may tell him she loves him but he can't understand why she continues to be so cold towards him. She will say, "Well, I have forgiven you but I haven't forgotten…" This is a thorn in his side. Actually, what she is trying to do is make him do penance. She has never truly forgiven him; if she had, she would not continually dwell on what happened.

Forgiveness for an act that is continually talked about is not true forgiveness. If one keeps reminding the other of the offense they have forgiven them of, they are only re-infecting the wound. To bring up a past wrong to your spouse means you *have not* forgiven. In the example that I used here, it could be the other way around and be an unfaithful wife also. Satan doesn't care which person is used to destroy a marriage.

If we say we will forgive but cannot forget, it's another way of saying we will not forgive. Of course, it's not easy to forget what has happened, but we can renew our minds and think on pure thoughts instead of the past. One person has said that forgiveness should be like a canceled note—it should be torn in two and burned so that it can never place anyone in debt again. Forgiveness that is half-hearted or partial is like a surgery that was never completed—it is actually worse than before.

If we feel proud or puffed up because of forgiveness, we may be apt to feel that the other person owes something for our forgiveness. Once again there has been no real forgiveness because there's been no real release.

The one who truly forgives eradicates or cancels the wrong of others as if it had never been done. We become willing to give up the debt with no mental reservations. In true forgiveness the debt is canceled—not because of generosity or because of moral superiority on our part, but because we realize we have not hated or condemned the person in the first place. When we decide to forgive, we realize there is nothing to forgive.

Don't condemn

One of the ways we can keep from getting hurt in everyday life is to keep our feelings under control. People will say and do adverse things to us as long as we live on earth, but we needn't condemn. Then there will be nothing to forgive. We can learn to separate the sin from the person.

There is an old saying about dealing with people: "A peach is not its fuzz, a toad is not its warts, and a person is not his or her sharp comments." As we learn to make the distinction, we will realize that it is Satan who is trying to destroy us.

In John 8 a woman who had been caught in the act of adultery was brought to Jesus by the Scribes and Pharisees. They wanted to stone her, but Jesus said, "He that is without sin among you, let him first cast a stone at her."

Those who heard Him were convicted of their own sins and began to walk away. Jesus said to the woman, "Where are those thine accusers? Hath no man condemned thee?"

She said, "No man, Lord."

Jesus said, "Neither do I condemn thee." Jesus did not condemn her, so He did not have to forgive. We can learn a valuable lesson when we see the influence of Satan in the hurtful things people may say or do. We are directed to pray for them, not condemn them.

> **Bless them that curse you, and pray for them which despitefully use you.**
>
> **Luke 6:28 (KJV)**

In other words, we turn the other cheek and go on as if nothing happened.

Forgive the debt

You may be bitter at someone for whom you have co-signed a note. They've not paid the bill and now you have to pay it. Forgive that person of that debt and go on with your life. Signing the note meant you were willing to take responsibility if that person did not pay. Of course, you felt they would pay or you would not have guaranteed the loan. It is painful to have to suffer through such an experience, but in light of the scriptures we have covered in this chapter, it's imperative that you release that person. Otherwise, strife is inevitable. The blessings of God are hindered because faith has been shut down.

The Bible instructs us not to guarantee someone else's loan. However, many believers are unaware of this scripture.

Be sure you know a person well before you vouch for his credit! Better refuse than suffer later.
Proverbs 11:15 (TLB)

Even if you know a person, it is still not advisable. Why? If you do and they don't pay, you are the one who will suffer later.

Unless you have the extra cash on hand, don't countersign a note. Why risk everything you own? They'll even take your bed!
Proverbs 22:26 (TLB)

Pardon

In order for us as believers to reach spiritual maturity, we have no choice but to forgive those who have wronged us.

Judge not, and ye shall not be judged: condemn not, and ye shall not be condemned: forgive, and ye shall be forgiven...

Luke 6:37 (KJV)

Jesus said when we forgive we would be forgiven. The word *forgive* here is from the Greek word *apoluo* which means to relieve, release, dismiss, let die, pardon, depart, divorce, let go, put away, and set at liberty. As we can see from these words, when we forgive we will forget. It will be as if nothing ever happened.

One word that has particular significance to me is *pardon*. When a person who committed a crime has been granted a pardon, that offender is restored and is given back his or her rights. It is as though the offense never happened.

A person who commits a crime and spends time in the penitentiary pays for the crime even after being released because it is still on the records. Many offenders lose their rights to vote, carry firearms or work on a government job. By law then, there is still a penalty to pay.

When we truly forgive someone, we pardon him. We let it die. It is put away or remembered no more.

And forgive us our debts, as we forgive our debtors.
Matthew 6:12 (KJV)

81

This word *forgive* comes from the Greek word *aphiemi* which means to lay aside, leave, put away, remit and yield up. Once again we see it means there is no holding on once we have forgiven a person. No matter who that person is, or what wrong was committed, forgiveness puts the sin away forever.

In Acts 7 Stephen had been stoned and was dying. His last words were, "Lay not this sin to their charge" (v.60). He totally forgave those who were taking his life. When we look at examples of forgiveness in the scriptures and compare them to today's situations, we see how Christians let small things cause division. Stephen asked the Lord not to put this on his murderers' accounts. When we are like Stephen and set people free, we are set free as well.

In Genesis 37, Joseph was sold to the Ishmaelites by his brothers because they did not understand him. He was called to be a leader and they were jealous. As a young man he was separated from his father whom he loved very much. Eventually he was put in prison. Yet when he became a man and was governor of Egypt with the power to destroy, he forgave his brothers when they came to him for help. He even gave them food.

Let's search our hearts continually to see if there is anything being held against another—a situation where forgiveness is needed. Let's walk together as one body united, with all walls broken down and free from the past!

Chapter 7
Walking in Love

Love is so much more than the expression of words. It is words, of course, but deeds and actions must be added as well. It's easy to love someone—even with deeds and actions—when love is returned. But few Christians come to the place of maturity where they can love the "unlovely." Jesus loved the unlovely because He controlled His emotions. He knew love dwelled inside Him and He chose to let love rather than His flesh rule.

We cannot trust our emotions. Emotions may change from minute to minute, but within our hearts we can trust the love of God—which *never* changes!

> **For I *am* the LORD, I change not; therefore ye sons of Jacob are not consumed.**
> **Malachi 3:6 (KJV)**

When people do or say things we disapprove of, or say things that tend to ridicule, the offense can be dealt with from the emotional level, or with the love of God. If we respond on an emotional level, we will never rise above the circumstances. However, if we respond through God's love, the entire situation will look different—we will rise above the emotional level and come out a winner.

Taking control of our emotions

One of the challenges we face after being born again is learning to take control of our emotions. Rather than seeing wrongs against us as an attack from Satan, we tend to see it as coming directly from the person. That attitude prompts us to retaliate or strike back. This reaction places us on the level with the person who committed the offense. It's a no-win situation. God's love abiding in us allows us to look beyond what is said and done. Human love cannot do this.

I read a story about Smith Wigglesworth's wife. Before the noted evangelist was saved he had told his wife she could not go to church. He threatened to lock her out of the house if she did. She felt she should go to church anyway, so she did. When she returned the house was locked as he had warned her. Because she could not get in and he would not get up and open the door, she stayed outside all night.

When he got up the next morning, he opened the door for her. She went in the house cold and tired, but did not speak of the inconvenience he had caused her. Instead, she lovingly asked him, "Smith, what would you like for breakfast?" It was by her attitude and resultant actions that he was moved, convicted and came to God. He became a great apostle of faith because his wife walked in love.

The power of God's love has not been made available to the person who is not born again. When an unsaved person faces an unpleasant situation there is no reserve of God's love to draw upon. That person must operate from a selfish viewpoint, protecting self.

I see many Christians who never mature in the love walk, and it is tragic. They never reach into their spirits and use the power of love that resides there. Instead, they continue to respond in a selfish way. Many of the hurts I experienced in my early walk with God could have been avoided if I had known more about this particular subject. When I was criticized or spoken evil of, I took it personally and fought back. This action was no different from the way I reacted before Jesus was my Savior. As a result, it caused hurt, pain and frustration for me and everyone else involved. My growth was hindered because of my attitude.

I was happy when revelation began to come to me about God's love and the power that I had within me. I learned I had control over my life and did not have to be affected by what was said or done to me. I could ignore it as if nothing had ever happened. This is God's plan for all believers. When this type of growth takes place, then the body of Christ will see true unity and be in one accord!

Where are we in the love walk?

As we grow in the Lord, we can ask ourselves searching questions such as:

Am I selfish?

Am I controlled by my emotions?

Do I always allow my feelings to be affected?

Do I cry every time something is said about me?

According to the Word of God these are childish reactions and Paul said to put away childish things. As we mature and grow up in love, we *can* change. When facing a particular problem, we needn't try to justify our actions or deeds. Looking at problems as Jesus would look at them allows Christ to be revealed in each one of us. We can overcome evil with good.

Though I speak with the tongues of men and of angels, and have not charity, I am become *as* sounding brass, or a tinkling cymbal.

1 Corinthians 13:1 (KJV)

Even the person who has a "silver tongue," always able to say the right thing, is unable to demonstrate love by words only. A person who uses the words, "I love you" may prophesy, preach, sing in the choir or have a special ministry, but these alone are not verifications of love. It is good that we say "I love you" often if we mean it, but the words must be backed up by action.

When someone has a need we are to demonstrate love to them by helping to meet the need—not just by making verbal expressions. Paul said if we don't do what is right our confession is merely a religious noise. The church has been religious too long. It is time to let love be at work.

Love is a decision

And this is his commandment, That we should believe on the name of his Son Jesus Christ, and love one another, as he gave us commandment.

1 John 3:23 (KJV)

Again we are told to love one another. It is a commandment and it is attainable. God would not tell us to do something that He has not enabled us to accomplish. We have been given the ability to love anyone and everyone at all times and in all situations. The more we act on this commandment the stronger we become in all areas of life. *All Christians can make the choice to love!* Love is a decision, not a feeling.

I've heard people say, "I just can't love so and so." They can't because they choose not to. The first step is to separate the person from the sin and then we see him or her as God does. This is not to say that we condone sinful acts, but we can still walk in love.

Ye are of God, little children, and have overcome them: because greater is he that is in you, than he that is in the world.

1 John 4:4 (KJV)

We are of God. He lives in us. Greater is He that is *within* us than he that is in the world. It is in Him that we live and move and have our being (Acts 17:28). In Him we can do all things (Philippians 4:13). Believers needn't rely on natural human power. It is not by our might, but by His love, His Spirit and His power that we overcome.

When we see a brother fall, God's love in us will go and pick him up. Instead of criticizing him and his faults or mistakes the believer will minister just as he or she would want to be ministered to. In a spirit of meekness we can restore our fallen comrade. We will forget about our own reputations and concentrate on being that hand extended.

Brethren, if a man be overtaken in a fault, ye which are spiritual, restore such an one in the spirit of meekness; considering thyself, lest thou also be tempted.

Galatians 6:1 (KJV)

Help those in need

How many times have we seen a brother or sister in need but we pushed it aside and said, "Someone else will help them. I'm too busy!" Love makes a special effort and goes out of the way to help those in need.

17 But whoso hath this world's good, and seeth his brother have need, and shutteth up his bowels *of*

compassion from him, how dwelleth the love of God in him? 18 My little children, let us not love in word, neither in tongue; but in deed and in truth.

1 John 3:17,18 (KJV)

God's love may be demonstrated by visiting the hospital to see a friend or loved one, spending time with an inmate in jail or showing kindness to someone who has lost a loved one. An expression of caring could change that person's entire life. As this scripture points out, it's not saying, "I love you," only; love means doing what we're able to do to help those in need.

In John 4 Jesus ministered to the woman at the well. He had to travel more than twenty miles out of His way but He did so that she might find truth. He gave her a drink of water—she would not thirst again. It was an act of love for Jesus to travel that distance; it was a sacrifice.

In Luke 10 Jesus told of a Jewish man traveling from Jerusalem to Jericho. The man was beaten, robbed and left for dead. A priest passed by and saw the man but would not help. A Levite also passed by and looked at the man but left him to die. However, there was a Samaritan on a journey who passed by the man. When the Samaritan saw the Jew who was left to die, he had compassion on him and forgot about his own busy schedule. He bathed his wounds, put him on his beast, took him to an inn and paid the bill. He told the host at the inn if the amount of money he was paying did not cover the bill, he would pay the remainder when he returned to that area.

This stranger took time to assist a man in need.

Many Christians today are so occupied with their own needs that they aren't willing to become involved with others. They live their lives at such a fast pace and with so many obligations they can't take time to get involved with other needs.

This is not obeying the commandment of love. We are to walk in love as the scriptures have described love. This means to open our hearts of compassion and take time to care for those around us.

Don't hold others in debt to you

Although I am not proud to tell this story I will because in the telling of it, others may be helped. A number of years ago I was traveling around the country holding meetings in large tents and auditoriums. My younger brother Norman came to work for me following his high school graduation. After working with me for a while, he was drafted into the service. While in the military service, he needed financial help, which I was able to give. Upon his discharge from the service, he came back to work for me as my tent manager.

On the whole, Norman did an excellent job. However, if he made a mistake, I would say to him, "After all I have done for you, how could you do this?" I really didn't realize what I was saying to him, nor did I realize that I was keeping him in debt to me.

We were having a crusade in Washington, DC, and I had come back to the tent after the night meeting (which I often did). I had this strange feeling that someone was going to try to steal our equipment. I went to my brother and said, "Make sure you and one of your men watch things tonight." He promised he would and told me to go on to my room and get some rest.

He stayed up for a while, but decided rather than get one of his men to patrol the area, he would do it himself. In the meantime, he went outside the tent to sit in one of the travel trailers for just a few minutes. Although he had no intention of doing so, he fell asleep. While he was asleep someone came and took all of our musical equipment, part of our public address system and other valuable items. Several thousands of dollars worth of equipment was taken and we had no insurance.

When I came into the morning meeting he met me and said, "I have bad news for you. I accidentally fell asleep last night and someone stole some equipment. When I woke up, it was gone."

"Norman," I said to him, "how could you let this happen after all I have done for you?"

"Wait a minute, Don," he retorted. "I've heard what you've done for me until I am tired of it. I'm guilty for not doing my job and I'll pay for it. You should be upset with me for neglecting my responsibility. But if I'm going to have to pay for your assistance while I was in the service for the rest of my life, then I wish you'd never helped me!"

That hit hard! I was stunned because I didn't realize what I had been doing. I grabbed him, threw my arms around him and repented of my wrongdoing. We were very close, but I had been driving a wedge between us. What I had done for him was given out of love, but I was unknowingly using it to keep him in debt to me.

He forgave me and never again did I mention to him what I had done for him. The only time that it has been thought of or spoken about is to tell others how they may be making the same mistake. Whether it is known or unknown, it needs to be dealt with.

How many times have parents been good to their children and kept them in debt? Love them unconditionally, train them properly, show them the right way, but give them the right to make their own decisions when they are able to do so. As children develop, they must be given room to continue growing. It is sometimes difficult for parents to back off and loosen the reins, but love will help give the space. When the time comes that they fall in love and are ready for marriage, godly love on the part of the parents will allow the children to go and live their own lives.

If during this process of growth children turn away from the things of God, don't confuse them with their sins. We are required to separate the two. We need not approve of or condone their wrong, but they must be assured of our love. *Love will win them back!* Nagging and complaining will only drive them farther away.

> **Train up a child in the way he should go: and when he is old, he will not depart from it.**
>
> **Proverbs 22:6 (KJV)**

When Christian parents live a godly life in front of their children and teach them the correct way, this scripture promise can be a strong anchor as the children grow and change.

Whatever they do, whether it is dating someone who is not of the faith, or hanging around the wrong crowd, parents can talk with them and remind them, with love, how the scripture tells them not to be yoked together with unbelievers (2 Corinthians 6:14).

It's vital during this time that they receive unconditional love, not nagging. If they become involved in drugs and alcohol, don't give up, but don't condone the sin either. They are still your children—don't disown them. Love them and you will win. Remember that you have God's love. His love does not wear down.

Love never fails or fades out

⁴Love endures long and is patient and kind; love never is envious nor boils over with jealousy, is not boastful or vainglorious, does not display itself haughtily. ⁵It is not conceited (arrogant and inflated with pride); it is not rude (unmannerly) and does not act unbecomingly. Love (God's love in us) does not insist on its own rights or its

own way, for it is not self-seeking; it is not touchy or
fretful or resentful; it takes no account of the evil done
to it [it pays no attention to a suffered wrong]. ⁶It does
not rejoice at injustice and unrighteousness, but rejoices
when right and truth prevail. ⁷Love bears up under
anything and everything that comes, is ever ready to
believe the best of every person, its hopes are fadeless
under all circumstances, and it endures everything
[without weakening]. ⁸Love never fails [never fades out
or becomes obsolete or comes to an end]. As for prophecy
(ᶦthe gift of interpreting the divine will and purpose), it
will be fulfilled and pass away; as for tongues, they will
be destroyed and cease; as for knowledge, it will pass
away [it will lose its value and be superseded by truth].

1 Corinthians 13:4-8 (AMP)

From verse 4 we can see there is no room for competition in the body
of Christ because God wants *all* His children to prosper. We should all be
working toward the same goals of winning the lost to Jesus and bringing
unity to the body. The Bible says promotion comes from God (Psalm
75:6,7). He will promote us and we will not have to compete with anyone!
It is so easy to become negligent and let our feelings be in control. But
when we let love work in our lives we will not be touchy or moody. I have
been around Christians who are so touchy and moody I never know what
to say to them.

In one of my camp meetings one of the speakers was ministering on
the subject of love. He said, "If several people were standing having
conversation together and one person invited only part of the group out
for fellowship at a restaurant or his home, those who were not invited
should not be offended but go on their way as if nothing ever happened."

We should always consider the feelings of others in a situation such as
this. This is only an illustration and should not take place, however. If for

some reason someone wanted to fellowship with only a few of the people in the group, he should wait until an appropriate time to invite them out for fellowship so as not to risk hurting others.

Have we grown to the place of not being offended yet? Probably not. We can begin to ask God to help us in the area because it's where so many let their guard down and let Satan cause havoc and confusion.

In the marriage relationship God's love must be practiced each day. Your spouse may not always be lovely, nor act lovely, but God's love will endure and will be patient with others. God's love as seen in 1 Corinthians 13:4-7 will not be puffed up, become arrogant, rude or insist on its own way. *Love gives!*

I have made this statement many times and it is true: "The one who gives the most or loves the most is the strongest."

In our society young men and women have been told, "Don't let your spouse have his or her way too much, or they will rule you."

First of all, that is carnal. When we operate in "God's love," we are *always* the winner! We don't count how many times we give because God's love bears up under anything and everything. God's love *never* fails or fades out!

We are not to love because of what someone does for us. We are to love unconditionally. Many Christians do not understand love. They enter into relationships for the wrong reason—many times to get. The right thing is to give. If you are expecting to get, and then don't—that is when you become offended. Many times the other person is not even aware of your expectations.

Over the years I've learned to love, not because of someone's kindness to me, but because God's love gives me the power to do so. Correct yourself.

Make sure you are measuring up instead of trying to get others to measure up. If someone is unkind or is not walking in love, don't condescend to repay.

Chapter 8
Giving

Learning to give is another important step in our spiritual development. We are to give our best to the Lord—our time, our talents, our money—all that we are and all that we have. In this chapter I will deal primarily with monetary giving.

The Bible has a great deal to say about money and giving—what attitudes and priorities we should have toward money and wealth; how much, when, where we should give; the blessings and dangers of riches.

Our attitude about giving is a strong indicator of our spiritual condition.

> [19]**"Don't store up treasures here on earth, where they can be eaten by moths and get rusty, and where thieves break in and steal.** [20]**Store your treasures in heaven, where they will never become moth-eaten or rusty and where they will be safe from thieves.** [21]**Wherever your treasure is, there your heart and thoughts will also be.** [22]**"Your eye is a lamp for your body. A pure eye lets sunshine into your soul.**
>
> **Matthew 6:19-22 (NLT)**

Right motives for giving

Give in order to honor God and express your love to Him

Giving is an act of obedience. It is one way to express our love and appreciation to the Lord.

> **Honor the LORD with your wealth and with the best part of everything your land produces.**
>
> **Proverbs 3:9 (NLT)**

Give to win the lost and help spread the gospel

Jesus is our example and He is the greatest giver—He gave His life. Our main motive and purpose for giving should be to win the lost and help in the spreading of the gospel.

> **14 How then shall they call on him in whom they have not believed? and how shall they believe in him of whom they have not heard? and how shall they hear without a preacher? 15 And how shall they preach, except they be sent? as it is written, How beautiful are the feet of them that preach the gospel of peace, and bring glad tidings of good things!**
>
> **Romans 10:14,15 (KJV)**

The time we give and the money we sow to help in a ministry make it possible for someone to be *sent* with the "Good News" of Jesus Christ! Money can build a church, pay for time on radio or television, send missionaries, or help with the salaries of the staff of those who are declaring the gospel of Christ. *Our gifts make all this possible!*

Anyone who is born again should have a desire to give towards the spreading of the gospel. Just think, someone gave and made it possible for us to hear. Now we should have that same desire to help the hurting. We may not be able to go out and spread the word, but we can give and send someone in our place.

¹⁴But how are people to call upon Him Whom they have not believed [in Whom they have no faith, on Whom they have no reliance]? And how are they to believe in Him [adhere to, trust in, and rely upon Him] of Whom they have never heard? And how are they to hear without a preacher? ¹⁵And how can men [be expected to] preach unless they are sent? As it is written, How beautiful are the feet of those who bring glad tidings! [How welcome is the coming of those who preach the good news of His good things!]

Romans 10:14,15 AMP

I have heard this statement made—"We are not responsible for the past generation, neither are we responsible for the future generation. But we, the Christians of today, are responsible for our generation." This statement is so true. It makes sense that the first priority of a Christian should be to let others know through the spreading of the gospel that Jesus Christ is Lord. When our lives have been changed by hearing the uncompromised truth, we should give to send the gospel of Christ around the world so that others may be helped as we were.

Wrong motives for giving

You have no doubt heard about people doing the right thing for the wrong reasons? That can happen when we give to the Lord. It is important to examine our motives for giving.

Don't give to receive recognition or appreciation.

¹"Take care! Don't do your good deeds publicly, to be admired, because then you will lose the reward from your Father in heaven. ²When you give a gift to someone in need, don't shout about it as the hypocrites do—blowing trumpets in the synagogues and streets to call attention

to their acts of charity! I assure you, they have received all the reward they will ever get. ³But when you give to someone, don't tell your left hand what your right hand is doing. ⁴Give your gifts in secret, and your Father, who knows all secrets, will reward you.

Matthew 6:1-4 (NLT)

It is important that we give to please God, not man. This is a vital principle in everything we do. We must strive to make all our choices, all our plans, based on what will please God, rather than what bring praise or rewards or honor from man.

Don't give out of obligation

Sometimes the leader of a service or someone meeting with you one-on-one might pressure you to give. Their intentions may be good, but they get over zealous in their plea. Don't allow anyone to pressure you to give. Consider what they say, but make a prayerful decision. Then be cheerful as you give. God loves a cheerful giver! The giving of ourselves, our time, and our money should never be done in bondage, but out of love.

Remember: A stingy planter gets a stingy crop; a lavish planter gets a lavish crop. I want each of you to take plenty of time to think it over, and make up your own mind what you will give. That will protect you against sob stories and arm-twisting. God loves it when the giver delights in the giving.

2 Corinthians 9:6-7(TMNT)

Paul is telling us in this scripture to be aware of the motive behind giving. He cautions us not to make a quick, impulsive decision but to take time to consider what we are doing. He says not to give because we feel sorry for someone, because there is a need, or because of someone putting the pressure on. If we do, we may regret it later. It is the cheerful, hilarious and excited giver whom God loves.

On the other hand, when we know God is prompting us to give, we should immediately respond in obedience. We are to be "joyous" and "prompt to do it."

Let each one [give] as he has made up his own mind and purposed in his heart, not reluctantly or sorrowfully or under compulsion, for God loves (He takes pleasure in, prizes above other things, and is unwilling to abandon or to do without) a cheerful (joyous, "prompt to do it") giver [whose heart is in his giving].

2 Corinthians 9:7 AMP

On occasion churches and Christian ministries may give a special appeal for a building project or some other special program or project. If the appeal is emotional, you may find yourself giving out of your emotions rather than listening to God's direction. Making a pledge for an amount too far above your faith level can result in a struggle that God never intended you to have. When you go beyond what God is telling you to do, you open yourself up to unnecessary struggle, anger and confusion. Often when people make a pledge based on an emotional response, they fail to pay the pledge. Each of us must purpose in our heart what we can do rather than being swayed by our emotions.

Sacrificial giving. Giving should not be a burden or strain, but a joy. The point here is not that we should avoid sacrificial giving. But we should never commit to giving which places us in bondage. The time to pray is *before* making the commitment. We must know where our faith level is and respond accordingly. If the funds aren't available, it's dangerous to commit just because others are. However, if God tells us to make a pledge even if the funds aren't available, He will provide it!

If God prompts you to give sacrificially or to make a pledge that appears to be beyond your means, be ready to take a leap of faith. This is the time to give sacrificially in obedience to the Lord. When He is leading you to give, you can be assured that He will make the way. He has a reason for leading you this way. As you obey Him, He will accomplish something within you. He will bring good results from your cheerful and trusting obedience.

> **God provides the seed. "¹⁰And [God] Who provides seed for the sower and bread for eating will also provide and multiply your [resources for] sowing and increase the fruits of your righteousness [ᶦwhich manifests itself in active goodness, kindness, and charity]. ¹¹Thus you will be enriched in all things and in every way, so that you can be generous, and [your generosity as it is] administered by us will bring forth thanksgiving to God. ¹²For the service that the ministering of this fund renders does not only fully supply what is lacking to the saints (God's people), but it also overflows in many [cries of] thanksgiving to God."**
>
> **2 Corinthians 9:10-12 (AMP)**

These verses of scripture reveal that God provides seed for the sower and He enriches us in all things and in every way so we can be generous givers.

When God tells us to give sacrificially and we are obedient, He will multiply our resources. Giving should be a joy. We are to give because we want to, not because we have to. Oral Roberts made an unparalleled statement when he said, "It's not a debt you owe; it's a seed you sow." God doesn't want us to go in debt by making a commitment before we think. We are to give only out of love. *You can give without loving, but you can't love without giving.*

Don't give to get

Although it is true that God will multiply back to us the gifts we give, this should not be the motive for giving. It pleases Him when a person gives from the heart with no strings attached.

Don't give in order to get blessings from God—or to put someone else under obligation. When we give our tithes and offerings, this does not give us a right to control those whom we support. If it is a gift from the heart, it is to aid the work of God and is no longer ours.

The amount of the gift is not as important as the attitude in which it is given. A person may give an offering of a thousand dollars, but a person who gave only ten dollars may have made the bigger sacrifice. If you gave a thousand in order to have a voice in church affairs, then the one who sacrificed to give ten should have a voice also. But no one should expect the right to have a voice solely on the basis of giving.

God has given the one in authority the vision for that ministry, and the gifts should go toward making that goal possible. Many good honest people have made the tragic mistake of thinking that because they tithe to their local church they should have a vote in how the money is spent. That is a wrong concept. The tithes are not ours—they are God's. When we give, we are giving back to God. Those whom we trust should have enough spiritual integrity to do with the money what God has told them to do. We give because we are being fed there, not in order to have a voice in leadership. A person who gives in order to gain some kind of control is giving for the wrong reason.

A person once told me he would purchase a piece of property for the church if I would change the name of it to one that he picked out. I could not do that. If God was telling him to purchase the property, he should have been willing to do it with no strings attached.

When giving into the kingdom of God, don't complain about it or impose your own stipulations on the recipient. We are to give freely into the kingdom of God. We release it just as a farmer releases the seeds he plants in the ground. He doesn't take them back or dig them up or complain about giving them. He leaves them there and waits until the seeds come up. He commits them to the ground.

²**People may be pure in their own eyes, but the LORD examines their motives. ³Commit your work to the LORD, and then your plans will succeed.**

Proverbs 16:2,3 (NLT)

Should I tithe?

Many people feel that tithing is a part of the law, and since they are no longer "under the law," tithing is not necessary. What they seem to overlook in the Word is the fact that the principle of tithing was instituted before the law was ever given. An example is Jacob's revelation of God's presence at Bethel in Genesis 28. He said in verse 22, "...**and of all that thou shalt give me I will surely give the tenth unto thee.**"

Another example is Abraham's tithe to Melchizedek in Genesis 14:20. Both of these acts took place many years before the law was given. This shows that the principle of returning to God a tenth of our blessings began even before Moses' day. When we give a tenth we are acknowledging God's blessings and demonstrating that we want to return a portion for the continual spread of the gospel and to express our thanks to Him for what He has done.

Under the law, the use of the tithe was not a national tax for Israel as some have said. The governing of Israel was accomplished through judges who were raised up as needed by the Lord from among many tribes or by kings who came from the tribe of Judah.

And all the tithe of the land, *whether* of the seed of the land, *or* of the fruit of the tree, *is* the LORD'S: *it is* holy unto the LORD.

Leviticus 27:30 (KJV)

And, behold, I have given the children of Levi all the tenth in Israel for an inheritance, for their service which

they serve, *even* the service of the tabernacle of the congregation.

Numbers 18:21 (KJV)

When God divided the land among the twelve tribes He gave the Levites no land to call their own. The tenth of all Israel was to be their pay because they were God's ministers.

26 Thus speak unto the Levites, and say unto them, When ye take of the children of Israel the tithes which I have given you from them for your inheritance, then ye shall offer up an heave offering of it for the LORD, *even* a tenth *part* of the tithe. 27 And *this* your heave offering shall be reckoned unto you, as though *it were* the corn of the threshingfloor, and as the fulness of the winepress.

Numbers 18:26,27 (KJV)

God was saying to the tribe of Levi that Israel was their field and if they ministered to it faithfully, tended to it well, and encouraged the people to do well, they were deserving of support. If they neglected their duties and Israel fell away from God, they were not deserving. The Levites prospered, as did the people, because their income was a percentage of the income of the people.

The tithe is mine. It has always been mine. You pay me by giving my tenth to the Levite who ministers to you.

Numbers 18:26,27 AP

God had more to say in Malachi about tithing and giving of offerings.

Bring ye all the tithes into the storehouse, that there may be meat in mine house, and prove me now herewith, saith the LORD of hosts, if I will not open you the windows of heaven, and pour you out a blessing, that *there shall*

103

not *be room* enough *to receive it.*

Malachi 3:10 (KJV)

As we tithe to honor God and to help spread the gospel, God promises to pour out abundant blessings. When we are faithful in tithing, He will bless us in ways we can't even imagine!

<u>**Tithing in the New Testament**</u>

Some people mistakenly believe that tithing is not taught in the New Testament. However, Jesus makes a clear reference to the fact that we should tithe.

> [23]**"How terrible it will be for you teachers of religious law and you Pharisees. Hypocrites! For you are careful to tithe even the tiniest part of your income, but you ignore the important things of the law—justice, mercy, and faith. You should tithe, yes, but you should not leave undone the more important things.** [24]**Blind guides! You strain your water so you won't accidentally swallow a gnat; then you swallow a camel!**

Matthew 23:23,24 (NLT)

Where Should I Tithe?

The tithe is the Lord's and should go into His work. Every Christian should have a home church where there is a steady diet of God's Word. If you are ministered to and receive spiritual training in your home church, that is the place where you should tithe regularly. If there is another ministry in which you are involved, one that helps equip you for the work of the ministry and ministers to your needs, you might want to prayerfully consider sowing part of your tithe into that ministry. As a general rule, however, all of your tithe should go to your home church.

How Much Should I Tithe?

By definition a tithe is 10 percent. I believe that Christians should tithe a tenth of their gross income. Income includes everything you receive—wages, housing or car allowance, gifts, inheritance, profit sharing and any other increase you receive.

Challenges

Some people have said, "Soon after we started tithing everything seemed to go wrong. We needed expensive car repairs, our old washer finally gave up and stopped working and our rent payment increased unexpectedly."

If you have had a similar experience it is important to recognize this as an attack from Satan. He does not want Christians to tithe and will do anything he can to stop us in the early stages of our commitment. He knows it will be harder for him to stop a believer whose faith is on a higher level. Instead of being discouraged when Satan tries to knock us down we need to recognize what is happening, rise up and keep on tithing. In the beginning of this book we talked about how we learn to walk as infants. Even though a toddler falls down many times he does not quit trying. He jumps right up and tries again and again. Apply this to the area of tithing.

When attacks come, some people let fear stop them from continuing to tithe. They couldn't meet their budget even before they started tithing—how can they possible tithe? But God has an answer—He challenges us to let Him prove the tithing principle to us.

[10]Bring all the tithes into the storehouse so there will be enough food in my Temple. If you do," says the LORD Almighty, "I will open the windows of heaven for you. I will pour out a blessing so great you won't have enough

room to take it in! Try it! Let me prove it to you!
Malachi 3:10 (NLT)

I encourage you to tithe consistently and faithfully. Don't give up if things seem difficult. Take that 10% out first—it belongs to the Lord! Trust Him and let Him open the doors of heaven for you.

Tithing on gifts

As a child I accompanied my family on visits to my grandmother. At Christmas and other special occasions we took gifts to her. She always asked us how much we paid for the gift.

I always thought my grandmother was being nosy or wanting to make sure we had bought her a good gift. My brothers and sisters and I would pool our money and get her the best gift we could afford—we wanted to make sure we could be proud of our purchase when she asked the inevitable question, "How much did you pay for this?"

My grandmother was a healthy person and lived to be 92 years old. When she went to be with the Lord, I (an adult now) sat on the front row at her funeral. As the pastor described her godly character and the fine example her life was to all of us, he began to describe her faithfulness in tithing. "Every time she received a gift," he explained, "she asked people how much they had paid for it so that she could be sure that she gave ten percent back to God."

At last, I understood. What a marvelous example my grandmother had set for us! I began to realize what an awesome heritage I enjoy. Not only was my grandmother a faithful tither, but my mom and dad tithed and taught me to do the same.

After this wonderful lesson from my grandmother's life I began to tithe on gifts as well—I encourage you to do the same.

Wise management

As explained above, financial problems can indicate an attack from the enemy. However, it is important to realize that sometimes there are other reasons why people have financial problems even when they are tithers and givers. Problems may be caused by poor management of funds or poor management of business affairs.

Examine your own situation. If poor management seems to be the problem I would recommend Christian financial counseling.

What about offerings?

The tithe belongs to the Lord. But the Word teaches us principles for giving offerings (gifts) over and above our tithes.

God favors a generous giver

> ⁶[Remember] this: he who sows sparingly and grudgingly will also reap
> sparingly and grudgingly, and he who sows generously [ᶦthat blessings may come to someone] will also reap generously and with blessings.
>
> **2 Corinthians 9:6 (AMP)**

Paul admonishes Christians not to be stingy with their substance. He exhorts us that when we sow generously in faith, God will also give back to us generously. If we sow sparingly and grudgingly, we should not expect God's blessing and favor. If we hold too tightly to what we have, we fail to learn God's principle for giving and to see supernatural power released in our lives.

It is possible to give away and become richer! It is also possible to hold on too tightly and lose everything.

Yes, the liberal man shall be rich! By watering others, he waters himself.

Proverbs 11:24 (TLB)

In 1963 Sharon and I were traveling on the evangelistic field. We were on our way to put up our small tent for a revival crusade and stopped at a tent meeting where a friend of mine was speaking. While talking with us he told us that he wanted to get a new tent. I looked around his tent and it seemed to be in perfect shape. I wondered why he would want another one.

Of course, I was comparing it with our tent. Ours was small and seated about 150 people. There were so many holes in it that when it rained people felt as if they were sitting outside instead of inside. I looked at the difference in size and condition of his tent to mine.

I thought to myself, "It sure would be nice to have a tent like this to work for God. I would be happy with one like this."

During the service he asked the congregation for an offering for his new tent. As he did I felt impressed to give one hundred dollars. I barely had a hundred dollars to get to our destination and put my little tent up. But I did not hesitate. Along with many others, I ran quickly to the front of the tent.

He received enough money to purchase the new tent. He then said, "Don, since you obeyed God, He is telling me to give you this tent." Was I ever excited then! I did not sow into his ministry because of a need that he had, but because God had impressed me to do so. It did not matter to me that he had more than I did. I gave the money because I wanted to and I believed God would bless us for sowing out of our need.

As we were leaving the service that night we did not tell anyone that we had several hundred miles left to travel with only a few dollars in my pocket. However, all at once people began to give us money. We received several hundred dollars as well as a new tent that would seat nearly 800 people. The minister also took his big truck and brought the tent to us. We gave generously and God rewarded us with favor because of our obedience.

> **And God is able to make all grace (every favor and earthly blessing) come to you in abundance, so that you may always and under all circumstances and whatever the need be self-sufficient [possessing enough to require no aid or support and furnished in abundance for every good work and charitable donation].**
>
> **2 Corinthians 9:8 (AMP)**

He did this for us—and He will do it for you. The saying that "you can't out give God" is so true.

God has a plan

When God calls us to give sacrificially, He has a reason. As we obey Him He accomplishes something within us. He will bring good results from our obedience.

> **Give, and [gifts] will be given to you; good measure, pressed down, shaken together, and running over, will they pour into [the pouch formed by] the bosom [of your robe and used as a bag]. For with the measure you deal out [with the measure you use when you confer benefits on others], it will be measured back to you.**
>
> **Luke 6:38 (AMP)**

Jesus said that when we give He will cause men to give back to us. When we measure out our gifts, they will come back in good measure, pressed down, and shaken together. The harvest may come in the form of money, or it may be favor with someone who will provide a job, or a promotion on a job, or a business opportunity. Remember that Jesus is saying that after we give, we can expect a return! This is a spiritual law. Sowing is followed by reaping.

Where our offerings should go

Our offerings can go into our home church and into other ministries. The main objective is that they should go into God's work.

Remember that all religious work is not God's work. God has instructed us to turn away from those who only have a form of God and do not have a true spirit of worship. Those who deny His power should not be included in our support.

Having a form of godliness, but denying the power thereof: from such turn away.

2 Timothy 3:5 (KJV)

Since we are admonished to turn away from those who are religious or have no depth in the things of God, our offerings should never be given to any organization that is not doing the same works that Jesus did. It is unscriptural to support so-called religious groups that are fighting, opposing or ridiculing a servant of God who is doing what Jesus called him to do. We should give tithes and offerings to the places where we are fed spiritually.

On several occasions I have asked people in my church if they were supporting other ministries. About fifty percent always responded that they did. Almost without fail, these were the ones who were greatly blessed. I encourage my members to support other ministries that are doing the work of God. I know that as they give, the windows of heaven are opened to them and God gives them more to give.

Giving to the poor

I believe in giving to the poor and to those who have needs. When we give to the poor we lend to God and He will give back much more than we have sown.

> **When you help the poor you are lending to the Lord—and he pays wonderful interest on your loan!**
> **Proverbs 19:17 (TLB)**

Follow the need?

People have told me, "Well, I'd like to support you. I come here regularly and you really do feed me, but I put my tithes and offerings where the greatest need is. Besides, you have more people to support you than so-and-so does, so I've been giving there."

If we give because of a need and not because we're being fed, it's *unscriptural.* It is all right to give when there is a need, but that should not be the only reason to give. Neither should a person have to always be made aware of a need before they give. I encourage giving to a need that will help hurting people, but we must be sensitive to God and give out of obedience. In this way, we will find joy in our giving. **I repeat—we mustn't rob our home church and the ministry where we're being fed to give to another need.**

> **Give, and it shall be given unto you; good measure, pressed down, and shaken together, and running over, shall men give into your bosom. For with the same measure that ye mete withal it shall be measured to you again.**
> **Luke 6:38 (KJV)**

Keep your commitments

God may speak to you to become partners with or make a commitment to a certain ministry. You respond and become a partner, but later change your mind and are not obedient to God. It is better not to make a commitment than to back out later. In this case, your mouth caused you to sin. We shouldn't make a commitment unless we mean it.

> **⁴When you vow a vow or make a pledge to God, do not put off paying it; for God has no pleasure in fools (those who witlessly mock Him). Pay what you vow. ⁶Do not allow your mouth to cause your body to sin, and do not say before the messenger [the priest] that it was an error or mistake. Why should God be [made] angry at your voice and destroy the work of your hands?**
> **Ecclesiastes 5:4,5 (AMP)**

God's will for you to prosper

God desires to meet *all* our needs. He wants us to live above and not beneath, to be the head and not the tail (Deuteronomy 28:13). When we are born again we become a part of *His* royalty, *His* wealth.

> **Let them shout for joy, and be glad, that favour my righteous cause: yea, let them say continually, Let the LORD be magnified, which hath pleasure in the prosperity of his servant.**
> **Psalms 35:27 (KJV)**

Some people think that to be a good Christian we must be poor. Others go to the opposite extreme and believe that if you have faith you will automatically be rich. Neither of these beliefs lines up with scripture.

Poverty Is Not a Virtue

It has been taught by some that we must be poor if we are Christians.

If ye be willing and obedient, ye shall eat the good of the land...
Isaiah 1:19 (KJV)

Lack of money prevents us from doing the things we dream of. Poverty prevents investment in God's work and prevents the gospel from being preached the way it should be. Poverty is a part of the curse of the law, and we've been redeemed from the curse through Jesus Christ. He took our poverty at Calvary and became poor that we might have plenty.

For you are becoming progressively acquainted with and recognizing more strongly and clearly the grace of our Lord Jesus Christ (His kindness, His gracious generosity, His undeserved favor and spiritual blessing), [in] that though He was [so very] rich, yet for your sakes He became [so very] poor, in order that by His poverty you might become enriched (abundantly supplied).
2 Corinthians 8:9 AMP

God is good, kind and generous. Jesus became poor so that we could have an abundant supply of what is needed. But we as believers must stand up for our rights. Don't let circumstances or Satan's lies keep you from your inheritance. Be a cheerful giver to God's work. Help those who are in need. Put God's plan first in all you do and you will reap abundant blessing.

When an earthly father sees his children do well, he is happy and rejoices with them. God is the same, and He has more than enough. He wants us to have more than enough also. Satan deceives and robs Christians of God's blessings by telling them it's not God's will for us to prosper. We have already touched on the fact that if money and material things have first place, then we are not in right relationship with God. Serving Him should have first place in our lives.

God does want the best for us

Becoming a Christian does not automatically bring about financial wealth, but it does open a door to abundant blessing.

> **Beloved, I wish above all things that thou mayest prosper and be in health, even as thy soul prospereth.**
> **3 John 1:2 (KJV)**

John says in this verse that he wishes above all things for Christians to prosper. Prospering is more than having material things. The complete meaning is having the power and ability to meet every need: *spiritually, physically, emotionally, financially and socially.* John indicates that our prosperity will come as our souls prosper. When our first priority is to seek and desire the material things of this world, our desires are selfish and will hinder godly blessings. This signifies a mind that has not been renewed to the things of God. Lust and greed will take over with unhappy results.

> **For the love of money is the root of all evil: which while some coveted after, they have erred from the faith, and pierced themselves through with many sorrows.**
> **1 Timothy 6:10 (KJV)**

We are to seek the kingdom of God rather than seeking wealth. As we seek God's kingdom and are obedient with tithes and giving, He will bless us.

> **But seek (aim at and strive after) first of all His kingdom and His righteousness ([His way of doing and being right), and then all these things taken together will be given you besides.**
> **Matthew 6:33 (AMP)**

114

God wants us to put Him first in all things. When we do, He gives us the things we desire. This does not necessarily mean that someone will give us everything. That is entirely possible, but He will more than likely give wisdom, knowledge, ideas and friends, things and people that can help us prosper.

But my God shall supply all your need according to his riches in glory by Christ Jesus.
Philippians 4:19 (KJV)

God will supply what we need by Jesus Christ. When we learn the principle of giving and seek to please God, the Lord will give us opportunity for great things. God does not bless us if we sit idly and wait for prosperity to come along. Some seem to think that if God wants us to have it, He will simply give it. No! It is when we go forward that God begins to move. He will open doors that may have been closed. He will guide our steps to the blessings that He has for each of us.

When we have the mind of Christ, the "things" we possess will not cause us to become puffed up. The more we have, the more humble we can become. We need to be shaped and changed by the Word of God—not by what we do or don't have.

Don't copy the behavior and customs of this world, but let God transform you into a new person by changing the way you think. Then you will know what God wants you to do, and you will know how good and pleasing and perfect his will really is.
Romans 12:2 (NLT)

God is our source

We don't have to get rid of material wealth, but we should not love or trust in money more than we do God. God is our source. We should not look to our bank account or our job or our business as our source. It is good stewardship to work hard and to do wise financial planning. God may choose to bless us through a job promotion, an unexpected gift or business success. But it is important to realize that **He alone is our source.**

> [17]**Tell those who are rich in this world not to be proud and not to trust in their money, which will soon be gone. But their trust should be in the living God, who richly gives us all we need for our enjoyment.**
>
> **1 Timothy 6:17 (NLT)**

There is a great deal of security in this teaching. Because God is our source, we don't need to be fearful if we lose our job or our business fails. God is always there—always the source of our blessing. It can be very difficult when we suffer a financial setback. It is important to get a grip on our emotions, remember who our source is, and be willing to trust Him.

Don't Be Satisfied With Mediocrity

Many people are satisfied with a car that runs, a roof over their heads, wearable clothes and being able to give a small amount to God. Don't be satisfied with being at or below the average. Get out of the rut, out of the "comfort zone." Take a giant step of faith and open that business, go after that promotion, work toward that raise, or buy that company so you can give more to God.

Perhaps you have never thought about owning your own business or rising above your present level of life. Trust God and ask Him for a dream. He will give you one and show you how it can be fulfilled to not only prosper you, but also to further the spreading of the gospel. When we take charge of our lives through the promises of God in His Word, He will join with us to take the kingdom by force (Matthew 11:12).

Does God return one hundred fold?

And Jesus answered and said, Verily I say unto you, There is no man that hath left house, or brethren, or sisters, or father, or mother, or wife, or children, or lands, for my sake, and the gospel's, But he shall receive an hundredfold now in this time, houses, and brethren, and sisters, and mothers, and children, and lands, with persecutions; and in the world to come eternal life.

Mark 10:29,30 (KJV)

Jesus said that we can receive the hundred fold in this life. Some things we should recognize about the hundred-fold return:

- The sowing and reaping are not limited to finances or material things. The sowing can be anything we give in service to Jesus and the spreading of the gospel: time, talent, relationships, home, money, etc. The hundred-fold blessing can also be in many forms (Jesus mentions house, brothers, sisters, parents, wife, children and land in this particular scripture.) I have many *spiritual* mothers, fathers, sisters and brothers. I have friends who own cottages and condominiums in different resorts and will let me stay there any time I want to. Actually, I would rather it be that way for me. Sharon and I have returns that come in many different ways and we are grateful for all of the benefits.

- Although God does want to give us the desires of our heart, begin where your faith level is. It is important to learn to trust God to meet your *needs* and grow into the area of *desires*.

God's plan first

God wants the best for us. He wants us to prosper and succeed. But He has a plan for each of us and along the way, as we strive to accomplish

His purpose for our journey (Genesis 24:12), there might be times of doing without, of making sacrifices.

God made the greatest sacrifice of all by giving His Son to die for us. How can we be unwilling to make any sacrifice that might be needed in the spreading of the gospel?

If pleasing God, if accomplishing His mission for us is truly our first goal, our greatest desire, then we can trust Him for the strength to be content in good times and in times of lack.

> **[11]Not that I was ever in need, for I have learned how to get along happily whether I have much or little. [12]I know how to live on almost nothing or with everything. I have learned the secret of living in every situation, whether it is with a full stomach or empty, with plenty or little. [13]For I can do everything with the help of Christ who gives me the strength I need.**
>
> **Philippians 4:11-13 (NLT)**

Paul experienced times of abundance and times of lack. But he never felt in need because his focus was on serving God, obeying Him, and winning souls. He knew that as he was faithful to God, Jesus would give him strength for any circumstances.

Hear God's Voice

God will always provide opportunities for us to sow. In 1970 I was speaking in Buffalo, New York, in the memorial Auditorium. I was staying with my in-laws just across the border in Canada. I traveled this route each day to the meetings. After the morning meeting I was on my way home when a voice inside me said, "Take the New York throughway."

Normally I took the route across the Peace Bridge into Canada, which was a shorter distance. I didn't pay much attention to the voice. Again and again, though, it said, "Take the New York throughway." Finally I said, "All right, I will take the throughway."

Just as I turned off on the throughway I saw there was construction work going on. I slowed my car almost to a stop. On my left I noticed a young couple along the road. Before I realized what I was doing, I put down the window and asked if they would like a ride. They accepted.

There was little conversation as I drove down the highway. As time passed I heard the voice of God again and He told me to give them some money. At first I didn't want to because I didn't know these people. I knew God had spoken, however, and as we got to the place where they were to get out I reached into my pocket and gave them all of the cash that I had with me. When I did, I told them the Lord told me to give it to them.

They looked surprised and the man said to his wife, "This is real money!"

I answered, "Yes, it is."

It was then that I learned their story. They had hitchhiked from Florida. Their house had burned and they lost everything they owned. With no insurance they saw no reason to stay and were returning to the area where they were originally from. They told me that several hours before I came along they had run out of money and had nothing to eat.

They took hands and prayed, saying that if there was a God like the One they had learned about in Sunday school, He would send help to them now. A little while later they went to a house and asked for food. The person at the house ran them off. This discouraged them and they had given up all hope that there was a God. They decided that it was no use to pray and didn't know what else to do. All at once, I stopped and picked them up—a total stranger. When I told them God wanted me to give them the money they were both touched.

As a result, on the New York throughway, they accepted Jesus into their hearts. Obedience caused two people to accept Jesus as Savior. I was rewarded on the spot for seeds that I sowed.

> **For God is the one who gives seed to the farmer and then bread to eat. In the same way, he will give you many opportunities to do good, and he will produce a great harvest of generosity in you.**
>
> **2 Corinthians 9:10 (NLT)**

Step out in faith

I encourage you to examine your own giving habits.

- What are your motives for giving?
- Do you tithe regularly?
- Do you give offerings over and above your tithe?
- Are you willing to give sacrificially when the Holy Spirit leads you to?
- Do you put God's plan for your life above all else?
- Are you always open to hear God when He directs you to give to a ministry, or to help an individual or family?

Are you ready to move to the next level in giving? Prayerfully consider your answers to these questions. Ask God for direction in moving to the next level—and then step out in faith!

> **This most generous God who gives seed to the farmer that becomes bread for your meals is more than extravagant with you. He gives you something you can then give away, which grows into full-formed lives, robust in God, wealthy in every way, so that you can be generous in every way, producing with us great praise to God.**
>
> **2 Corinthians 9:10 (TMNT)**

Chapter 9
Patience

Many Christians listen to teaching tapes, read Christian books, go to meetings and hear testimonies of what God has done for others. They get excited and want to be full-grown immediately. They expect all of the things they are praying and believing for to happen *now*!

To obtain the things that we desire we must first understand how faith works. Faith is not a magic wand to bail Christians out of crises or to deliver overnight success. Faith is a way of life. It is the trust and confidence in God that He will keep His Word. Faith is gained and developed by putting it into practice. Patience is a key factor in using faith to its fullest extent.

Patience is having the ability to stand and wait without complaining. It means being steadfast, enduring, persevering and unmovable from the truth of the Word. W.E. Vine's Dictionary says that patience is the quality that does not surrender to circumstances or succumb under trial. It's the lack of patience that many times keeps Christians from receiving God's blessing.

Faith is like a seed

The farmer is an example of patience. He plants seeds in the spring and waits until the end of summer or the beginning of fall for the harvest. He doesn't give up—he simply waits until harvest time. Have you every prayed for something and then given up because you have not physically seen the answer soon enough? This waiting period should be a time not to give up, but to renew the vision, trust God and stand firm. Don't let Satan steal what belongs to you; he can only take what you let him take. *God is your source!*

When a seed of corn is planted it does not become fully grown overnight. First the little blade begins to break through the soil. If we were to watch it closely from day to day we could not actually see it growing, but it keeps getting taller and taller. On the package of seed it says it will take from 80 to 120 days before the corn is ready for harvest, so we must wait. Receiving from God is just that simple. We must give God's Word time to grow inside of us in order to produce what we've asked for. Faith is like a seed. It must be given time to grow.

26 And he said, So is the kingdom of God, as if a man should cast seed into the ground; 27 And should sleep, and rise night and day, and the seed should spring and grow up, he knoweth not how. 28 For the earth bringeth forth fruit of herself; first the blade, then the ear, after that the full corn in the ear.

Mark 4:26-28 (KJV)

A couple of weeks after you've planted the corn you go out to look at it and become excited because you see the blades breaking through the earth. Even though it is not fully matured, what do you call it? Corn, of course. When you show your plants to someone you say, "Let me show you my corn." It is not corn yet, but you are already calling it corn and the plant will produce corn. You are actually "calling those things that be not as though they were."

This is what patience will do for us as believers. When we have patience we will wait without giving up or becoming discouraged.

Don't Let "No" Stop Your Success

The statement "no" does not always mean there's no answer to what we're believing for. You may have applied for a job only to find that the company has hired someone else. Don't give up and get discouraged because someone else was hired. Go back again! That person who was hired may not like the job and quit, or be fired. People leave jobs every day by resigning, being terminated, transferring and retiring. There are always openings somewhere. Be patient! Fill out another application and tell the prospective employer you want the job. Be persistent and claim God's favor. Don't be bashful. Go with confidence and God will go with you.

My younger brother came to a Sunday morning service where he heard me teach on "Persistence and Patience." He had a job at the time but was not satisfied with it. He had filled out applications in different places and he was called to interview for a job that he really wanted. When he arrived he was told that they had just hired someone for that position. However, he did not take that response as the final answer. He told the personnel office, "I want to leave my resume with you." The response was that there would be no purpose in his doing so.

Trusting in God rather than in what he was told, my brother convinced them to let him leave his resume. In spite of the opposition facing him, he left the building praising God. The next day he was called to come into work! The person they had hired quit the job after the first day. My brother's patience and persistence, along with faith in God, obtained the job that he wanted. Be patient and persistent. Don't give up—God has exactly what you have requested!

Don't be discouraged

35 Cast not away therefore your confidence, which hath great recompence of reward. 36 For ye have need of patience, that, after ye have done the will of God, ye might receive the promise.

Hebrews 10:35,36 (KJV)

When we lose hope we lose confidence and become discouraged. I have watched people lose hope because of circumstances—perhaps a divorce, the loss of a job or other types of dilemmas in their lives. If you are in that place today, don't despair.

Let your **conversation** *be* **without covetousness;** *and be* **content with such things as ye have: for he hath said, I will never leave thee, nor forsake thee.**

Hebrews 13:5 (KJV)

This is a promise. Believe it and hold on to it. After we have done all we know to do, it's time to exercise patience and stand.

We all have opportunities to lose hope and give up. But God has given His grace to help us win and to overcome discouragement.

Satan will try to discourage us through circumstances. The word "discourage" means to deprive of courage, hope or confidence; dishearten; to advise or persuade a person to refrain; to try to prevent by disapproving or raising objections or obstacles. When you step out in faith, well-meaning people, including Christians, will advise you not to attempt what you have planned. They will tell you how they tried the same thing, or something similar, and failed and will raise objections to dishearten you. All of this is the work of Satan to get you to lose courage and confidence. This is where patience comes in. We are told we can encourage ourselves in God's Word even though we may not feel like it.

In 1 Samuel 30 we see how David encouraged himself. He was distressed because the city had been burned. His two wives and children, along with his men and their wives and children, had been taken captive. After he prayed God told him to *pursue, overtake and recover all.*

It was because David had encouraged himself that he was able to move forward. God gave David the strength and He will do the same for every believer. When we encourage ourselves, we will hear the voice of God. God will give direction. When we give in to discouragement, God's voice is dim. To encourage means to give courage, hope or confidence, to give support to.

As David encouraged himself in the Lord, courage, hope and confidence came to him. He also received the support of his men to go with him to recover their families. Meditation and confession of God's Word are encouraging and bring new hope and confidence.

7 Only be thou strong and very courageous, that thou mayest observe to do according to all the law, which Moses my servant commanded thee: turn not from it *to* the right hand or *to* the left, that thou mayest prosper whithersoever thou goest... 9 Have not I commanded thee? Be strong and of a good courage; be not afraid, neither be thou dismayed: for the LORD thy God *is* with thee whithersoever thou goest...

Joshua 1:7,9 (KJV)

Webster's Dictionary defines *courage* as the attitude of facing and dealing with anything difficult or painful instead of withdrawing from it. Courage is the quality of being fearless, brave or valiant. God was making a point that when we are faced with difficult situations or when something is painful, we aren't to withdraw from it, but we are to be strong and fearless. In other words, we are to encourage ourselves in the Lord.

For I am with you wherever you go. Don't look at the circumstances on the right or on the left, but remember my promise that I will prosper you wherever you go.

Joshua 1:9 AP

God is speaking the same thing to us today—by faith and patience we will inherit His promises.

Patience at work

When Moses sent out the spies in Numbers 13:20, he told them to be of good courage. The word *courage* here from the Hebrew word *chazaq* means to conquer, be consistent, continue, fortify, hold fast, be mighty, be stout, be sure, be urgent, withstand.

Again we can see patience at work here because as Christians we are to be constant in our faith and confession. As we continue walking with God we can be sure God means what He says and we can withstand the pressures Satan brings. We are stout with God's power; we are mighty in the face of all opposition; the Word of God fortifies us and brings us through every situation.

God told Joshua to be strong and of good courage. God was telling him he could stand and be an overcomer every day of his life, and we can too! Webster's Dictionary defines the word *strong* as tough, able to resist attack, not easily defeated, not weak, but forceful, persuasive, active.

The believer who develops patience will stand firm and resist the attacks of the enemy. The person with patience stays active and forceful, showing no signs of weakness, but presses through with total confidence in God's Word. Patience is the force that keeps us from veering off to the right or left of what we are believing for.

Faith and patience —
a winning combination

The Word of God is our title deed to the answers. It is all we will ever need. Whatever you are standing in faith for, continue standing. God is faithful to His Word and He hastens to perform it (Jeremiah 1:12). As we hear and do His Word we will not be moved by Satan's greatest attacks, but will stand steadfastly, and the power of God will break the yokes.

¹⁴Stand therefore [hold your ground], having tightened the belt of truth around your loins and having put on the breastplate of integrity and of moral rectitude and right standing with God, ¹⁵And having shod your feet in preparation [to face the enemy with the firm-footed stability, the promptness, and the readiness produced by the good news] of the Gospel of peace.¹⁶Lift up over all the [covering] shield of saving faith, upon which you can quench all the flaming missiles of the wicked [one].
Ephesians 6:14-16 (AMP)

Attacks and trials from the enemy do not cause us to have patience. They cause us to use or work the patience we already have. If we go after something in faith we must make the decision to stand until the answer comes. If this decision is never made, the attacks will then cause us to lose sight of what we are believing for.

When we put patience to work, tighten the belt of truth and stand firmly on the Word, in spite of the attack of flaming darts, our faith and patience withstand them all. We will be more than conquerors! We can win—we are winners! A winner never quits and a quitter never wins. Whatever we are believing for—an unsaved spouse, son, daughter, parent to be saved, we need not let Satan cheat us. We can reign in life! We are heirs of God and joint-heirs with Jesus.

As a pastor I have had to tighten the belt of truth and walk in patience. Attacks have come and situations have looked impossible, but when I stand on God's Word, victory always comes. It may not be according to my timetable, but His timing is always perfect.

Several years ago we were buying a building for our church and needed the entire amount of money by a certain date. We had already invested several thousand dollars and it seemed we had come to the end. We did not have the money to close the deal, which meant we would lose all we had invested. The day came when we were supposed to complete the agreement.

I sat at my desk and said, "Lord, I'm not worried about this situation. You will come through for us, I know You will." I brushed the problem aside and went about my day. Later that day the man from whom we were buying the property came by.

"I am having a problem with the papers," he told me. "I can't get a clear deed. It looks as if it will take me ninety days to complete it."

This was the answer to my prayer because the additional ninety days gave us the time we needed to raise the extra money. I did not perceive that he would have a problem but I stood anyway. God moved for me in a mighty way, not by giving me the money on that date, but by giving me more time. At the end of the ninety days we were ready and closed the deal.

3 Knowing *this*, that the trying of your faith worketh patience. 4 But let patience have *her* perfect work, that ye may be perfect and entire, wanting nothing.
James 1:3,4 (KJV)

My faith was tried, but patience was at work and the victory was won.

A businessman in my church had been bidding on a very large contract. He had spent many hours preparing the bid, plus the time he traveled from his office to theirs. He was patient and believed he was going to get the contract. He was sure of it! The news came that the contract was given to another company. Needless to say, he was disappointed about the whole thing. Instead of falling into despair, he remembered a message I had taught, ""Stand Up and Live." He began to encourage himself with the Word. Faith, confidence and hope rose up within him.

He called the firm and told them that he would like for his company to do the installation on this project. They were surprised that he would call and even talk to them, much less ask to do the work. His attitude was positive and they called him back to do the installation. The job turned out to be the biggest job his company had ever done up to that point. As an added benefit, the negotiating experience and business contacts he obtained through this deal later brought him a contract for over two million dollars.

He could have become angry and given up, especially after all the hours he had put into the contract. Instead, he chose to stand up and love. When he did, God gave him favor and the job was won.

Don't Be Afraid

Another of Satan's weapons against the believer is fear. Actually he tries to intimidate us with his attacks. He would prefer for Christians to worry rather than rest in the Lord.

> **Come unto me, all *ye* that labour and are heavy laden, and I will give you rest.**
>
> **Matthew 11:28 (KJV)**

When we walk in the light of the Word Satan may threaten, but we need not be intimidated by it. The word *intimidate* means to make timid, or to cow down, to force or deter with threats of violence. When we walk and live by faith, Satan will always attempt to intimidate us. In other words, he threatens us with circumstances, putting negative thoughts in our minds, trying to get us and other Christians to act timid and to cow down to him.

When we let his threats take hold, despondency comes. We lose courage, hope and confidence. We lose patience and Satan moves in. Prayers go unanswered and we turn to self-pity. "I don't understand why this has happened to me," we may lament. "I've stood, I've prayed, I've confessed, but look at me—no one even cares." The problems came as a result of listening to Satan's lies.

We can choose to put the Word to work and stand our ground!

> **... but he that is begotten of God keepeth himself, and that wicked one toucheth him not.**
>
> **1 John 5:18 (KJV)**

God has given believers a way to protect or keep ourselves from the threats of Satan. We are begotten of God—Satan can't touch us unless we let him. God has not given us a spirit of fear, but a spirit of love and a sound mind. Perfect love will cast out any and all fear.

> **Fear not [there is nothing to fear], for I am with you; do not look around you in terror and be dismayed, for I am your God. I will strengthen and harden you to difficulties, yes, I will help you; yes, I will hold you up and retain you with My [victorious] right hand of rightness and justice.**
>
> **Isaiah 41:10 AMP**

As we continue to encourage ourselves in the Lord, we are strengthened. As we exercise patience, we are better able to withstand difficulties. As we walk by faith and not by sight, we look at the end results rather than the problems and difficult situations. Even though the present situation may seem insurmountable, we know the Spirit of God is bringing change to the situation.

> **... first the blade, then the ear, after that the full corn in the ear.**
>
> **Mark 4:28 (KJV)**

It takes time for faith to produce the end result. We must give the answer time to come and meanwhile not let Satan bring fear and timidity. Plant the seed of faith. Water it by meditating and praying the Word, and it will grow to maturity—but not overnight!

We needn't succumb to fear. God is faithful. He has given believers His faith, His power, His love, His wisdom and His Spirit.

> **For God hath not given us the spirit of fear; but of power, and of love, and of a sound mind.**
>
> **2 Timothy 1:7 (KJV)**

Fear is not of God. Fear is meditating and worrying about the things that we don't want to happen. God does not give fear but love, confidence and hope. So why listen to Satan's threats?

> **Finally, brethren, whatsoever things are true, whatsoever things *are* honest, whatsoever things *are* just, whatsoever things *are* pure, whatsoever things *are* lovely, whatsoever things *are* of good report; if *there be* any virtue, and if *there be* any praise, think on these things.**
>
> **Philippians 4:8 (KJV)**

Satan wants Christians to doubt God's ability to keep His Word and thus hinder our faith and patience. But if we meditate on the answer and are persistent and give God time to work in our behalf, the answer will come. There is a time and a season for everything.

Many believers want things to happen immediately and then give up if they don't see a physical change overnight. A building is not built overnight, and a child is not developed overnight. I am not inferring that we should expect many months or years to pass before we see results. We can expect it *now* and see it *now*. When we take a stand on God's Word, we can watch it develop. Some things take time for faith to develop or mature.

I believe many pastors have been discouraged because they saw the seeming "instant success" of other pastors. Their churches may be small and their growth minimal when compared to others. It is a mistake to look at another church, city or state and compare yours to theirs. If you are in that position, it may be wise to see what a "successful" pastor is doing. Perhaps you are making mistakes that are hindering your growth. Perhaps the pastor of the faster-growing church is reaping seed that has been sown by others. The pastor of the slower-growing church may have to first plow up the fallow ground of tradition and religious spirits before he can begin to sow in good soil. Perhaps no pastor taught the uncompromised Word in that area before.

As has been said before, faith and patience will surely pay off. If you are a pastor or member of a church that is not growing as fast as others, and if you are doing all you know to do, don't become discouraged. Your seeds will come up! Everything we say is a seed. Every radio spot, every newspaper ad, everything is a seed! It may not come up for years, but it will come up. Don't be in a hurry—we always reap.

When I first moved back to Chattanooga, Tennessee, I decided to begin an exercise program and I joined a local health spa. I told the instructor that I wanted a larger chest, smaller waist, stronger legs and bigger biceps, but I didn't want a big neck.

He measured me, weighed me and prescribed the proper regimen. He said, "I want you to start with this program and as you get used to it, we will increase the weight and number of repetitions."

I agreed and went to the gym floor where he took me through each set of exercises. At the end he said, "You're finished for the day. You can go to the steam room and whirlpool—I'll see you day after tomorrow."

When we finished I didn't feel tired or out of breath. I looked around and saw those who had been on a program for several years. Everywhere I looked I saw people who had developed powerful muscles. I looked at them and then at myself.

I said to myself, "I need a better workout. I haven't done enough." I went back to the weights, added more, did more repetitions, then flexed my muscles in the mirror. I did this repeatedly. I could just see myself getting larger, but as I continued I became so weak my legs shook when I walked.

I went to the steam room and the whirlpool. By the time I got out of the whirlpool I could barely make it to the shower. After I dressed I struggled to the snack shop and asked for a drink that would give me some energy. I was weak and felt terrible! After a few minutes, I finally made it to the car.

When I arrived home Sharon said, "What happened to you?"

I said, "I got muscles."

I had to lie down to regain my strength. I also had to drink more and eat just to sit up. By bedtime I was feeling a little better. I went over to the mirror, pulled off my t-shirt and began to flex my muscles. I said to Sharon, "Look how big my chest and biceps are!"

She replied, "Why don't you go to bed." She was not very impressed.

Needless to say, when I got up the next morning the only thing that would move were my eyelids. I was so sore Sharon had to help me get out of the bed. I was in so much pain I sat in a hot tub for thirty minutes before I could walk.

Obviously, I was trying to obtain muscles overnight. I learned the hard way that it does not come that way—it takes time! I had been told what to do and I knew better, but I ignored my instructor and consequently suffered. He showed me the proper way to keep me from getting sore and wearing out, but I wanted muscles *now*! Even though I did extra exercise and went through much pain, it did not help. I only felt worse.

The point here is to take God's Word and apply it every day. Give the Word time to grow inside you and let patience have her perfect work. The result is that you will be fully equipped, wanting nothing! Patience must be active in the life of the believer for him or her to come into maturity. Have a plan for prayer and Bible study. Continue to follow it and you will be able to stand because of your faith and patience.

Chapter 10
The Importance of Prayer

Prayer should not be looked upon as an obligation or something that a Christian must do. Prayer is an opportunity—something we are privileged to be able to do. Prayer should not be put off or dreaded. It should not become bondage to any believer. By praying, we are in communication and in fellowship with God. We should look forward to prayer, just as we look forward to spending time with our families. When our family spends an evening together it is a great opportunity to be together and enjoy one another's company.

I rise early most every morning and pray because of a desire to spend time with the Father—not out of obligation. As I do so, my relationship with God is strengthened, my vision is renewed and I am greatly encouraged.

To develop into mature Christians we must recognize the importance of prayer and place it high on our priority list. The mature Christian understands that prayer is a vital part of his or her walk with the Lord. Those who dread to pray or put it off have never learned how to communicate or fellowship with God. To them, prayer is labor. To the spiritually mature Christian, prayer time is the most refreshing, rewarding time of the day.

There are those who say, "I pray all the time—when I'm riding in my car on the way to work or to church." I agree that this is good and don't stop if you do this, but also set aside quality time each day that is just between you and the Father. If you are married, you do not talk to your spouse only when you're traveling in the car. A strong relationship between a husband and wife is built by the quality time spent sharing with one another.

I encourage all Christians to develop a consistent prayer life. Cultivate daily times of prayer. Just as we eat regularly to have strength to go through the day, so must we have regular times of prayer to strengthen us in the Spirit. We don't eat out of obligation—most people enjoy eating. Prayer should be the same way in the life of every believer.

I am a praying person. That is not a boastful statement, but because I pray I feel qualified to encourage others to do the same. I was born again when I was fifteen years old. My mother was a praying person. She loved to pray and did so right up until the time she went home to be with Jesus. I learned to pray from my mother. Prayer works!

How do I pray?

And in that day ye shall ask me nothing. Verily, verily, I say unto you, Whatsoever ye shall ask the Father in my name, he will give *it* you.

John 16:23 (KJV)

Jesus was saying here that after the resurrection we can't physically ask Him anything, but whatever we ask the Father in Jesus' name, He (God) will give it.

Anything we ask should be done in Jesus' name. The name of Jesus is the key that unlocks the door. When we understand the power and authority in His name, we can see all of heaven standing to attention when we pray in the name of Jesus. E.W. Kenyon once said, "When we pray in the name of Jesus it is the same as if He were here doing the praying Himself."

> **And whatsoever ye do in word or deed, *do* all in the name of the Lord Jesus, giving thanks to God and the Father by him.**
>
> **Colossians 3:17 (KJV)**

Each time we come to the Father for anything, we should pray in Jesus' name, not for Jesus' "sake." Using the name of Jesus in everything we do is like having power of attorney. In other words, as Christians, the name of Jesus has been given to us to use in prayer. When we pray in Jesus' name our prayers are received by the Father because the name of Jesus is our legal entry into the throne room.

Pray by faith

I've heard people say, "I pray, but when I do it feels like I'm hitting a brick wall."

Think about that statement for a moment. What difference does it make what it "feels" like? The Bible does not say God hears us when we "feel" like He does. We come to Him, not by our feelings, but by what we believe. Whether or not we feel anything has no bearing on whether God hears.

When we come to the Father in Jesus' name, He always hears us. Before Jesus raised Lazarus from the dead, He prayed this prayer:

> **41 Then they took away the stone *from the place* where the dead was laid. And Jesus lifted up *his* eyes, and said, Father, I thank thee that thou hast heard me. 42 And I knew that thou hearest me always: but because of the people which stand by I said *it*, that they may believe that thou hast sent me.**
>
> **John 11:41,42 (KJV)**

Just as Jesus said, "I know that thou hearest me always…" the mature Christian should know that prayers are always heard when prayed in faith and according to the will of God.

> **14 And this is the confidence that we have in him, that, if we ask any thing according to his will, he heareth us: 15 And if we know that he hear us, whatsoever we ask, we know that we have the petitions that we desired of him.**
>
> **1 John 5:14,15 (KJV)**

When our prayers are in agreement with God's Word, our petitions are not selfish. We can have the confidence that our prayers are heard and that we will receive what we ask for. It's that simple.

> **Therefore I say unto you, What things soever ye desire, when ye pray, believe that ye receive *them*, and ye shall have *them*.**
>
> **Mark 11:24 (KJV)**

In this verse Jesus tells us we can have what we desire if we believe. When we pray we must ask in faith, without wavering (James 1:6).

Pray for those in authority

> **1 I exhort therefore, that, first of all, supplications, prayers, intercessions, *and* giving of thanks, be made for all men; 2 For kings, and *for* all that are in authority; that we may lead a quiet and peaceable life in all godliness and honesty.**
>
> **1 Timothy 2:1,2 (KJV)**

Paul exhorts Christians to pray for government leaders because they have great responsibilities. We should pray that they will demonstrate integrity, walk in wisdom, deal wisely in all issues and help ensure that freedom will be maintained in our country.

We are to pray that laborers will be sent to witness and minister to those in authority who are not born again. Also pray that men and women of God give wise counsel to them. Kings in the Old Testament called upon the prophets and many times God sent them with a message to the king. I believe it can be the same now.

We should pray that leaders who govern unjustly will be confused and that God will raise up new ones to replace them. Pray that those who oppose God and His Son Jesus will fall from their position of power.

> **Destroy thou them, O God; let them fall by their own counsels; cast them out in the multitude of their transgressions; for they have rebelled against thee.**
> **Psalms 5:10 (KJV)**

One of the ways revival will come to nations is by government leaders having an experience with God. Paul said to pray for those in authority, and this includes those in the ministry. I believe Christians should pray for their pastors every day. Pray that your pastor walks in the spirit of wisdom and the revelation knowledge of Jesus, that his eyes will be enlightened by the Holy Spirit always to do the will of God.

The four other ministry gifts are as important to the body of Christ as the pastor and should be included in our prayers also. Pray that there is perfect love among those who operate in the five ministry gifts. Pray that there be no competition or strife, but that all work in unity to accomplish the will of God in their lives and in the body of Christ.

Satan attacks the men and women of God who are in the ministry and they need our prayers. Pray that they will not be caught off guard when attacks come, but that they will recognize what Satan is trying to do and not let him in. The five ministry gifts have been placed in the body to lead and minister depth in God's Word. As we pray for them, God will use them in a greater way to minister to the needs of the Church.

Pray for others

It is important for Christians to have compassion and concern for others and pray for the needs of others to be met. As we give to others by praying for them, healing will come to us. Or the answer to our needs will manifest. Or both. It's a spiritual law. When we pray for others, God will cause others to begin to pray for us.

Confess your faults one to another, and pray one for another, that ye may be healed. The effectual fervent prayer of a righteous man availeth much.

James 5:16 (KJV)

Praying for others actually causes faith to grow. As we release faith for the answer, we become excited about the needs of others being met. As a result, we see the answers to our own needs being manifested.

Paul tells us in Ephesians 6:18 to pray for all saints. Many believers will pray for their families, their circle of friends and ministries that they know. However, God wants us to have a larger vision and express love and compassion to more than a small circle.

God wants us to pray for those in other denominations, people we don't even know. Get involved and concerned in prayer about ministries that have not yet been Spirit-filled or groups with whom you do not agree. Pray for them and God will minister to them.

Everywhere I go people come up to me and tell me that they pray for me all the time. It blesses me. I know why my name is placed on their hearts. It's because so much of my prayer time is spent praying for others.

Many times as I have gone to prayer I have been hurting and aching inside. However, instead of focusing on my needs, I gave attention to the needs of people in my church, others I've known in the ministry, friends, neighbors and many whom I did not know well. When I finished praying for them, the hurt would be gone. It was released as I prayed for others. Oh, what a joy to pray!

Spending quality time in prayer, fellowshipping with God and praying for others are areas in which I have matured a great deal. I have been drawn closer to many people because of the time I spend in prayer for them. I have watched other people who have had a bad attitude toward me change as I spent time with God praying His best for them.

If you have not developed a regular prayer time, I encourage you now to put aside time each day for prayer. Don't wait until the end of the day or the evening for your time with the Lord. You will be too tired then and probably too sleepy. Pray when you are fresh and alert. Give your best to the Lord. As you start your day with prayer, it will keep you in agreement with the Word of God all day long.

When we make a commitment to prayer, we will be more concerned about those around us through the day because each time we talk to people we've prayed for, we are reminded of our prayers. This causes us to encourage them, and as we encourage others we are edified.

Have a prayer list

When praying, make a list of the people who need prayer and jot

141

down the reasons. Rather than simply asking God to "bless so-and-so," be specific. God has already blessed the believers with all spiritual blessings (Ephesians 1:3), but we must know how to bring these blessings into fruition. A prayer list keeps us from forgetting what we should pray for. Follow the list unless the Spirit leads otherwise.

Try to avoid looking at the clock every few minutes to see how long you have prayed. Set aside a specific amount of time for prayer and give that time to God. When I pray at home I have a room where I go and I do not take a clock. The time goes by quickly because my mind is not on the time but on fellowshipping with God.

Make a commitment to pray a certain amount of time each day. If the commitment is fifteen minutes, perhaps you can stay an extra five minutes, but the commitment has been for only fifteen minutes.

As this regimen begins to take hold, raise the commitment five more minutes. I started with an hour and stayed an extra fifteen or twenty minutes—sometimes even an hour. I committed to what I knew I would keep and prayer became a beautiful part of my life.

This chapter on prayer is not intended to teach on different kinds of prayer, but to encourage Christians to incorporate prayer as a daily routine to develop Christian maturity. We will discuss some of the more important areas of prayer.

A prayer list is effective, but we're not bound to it or by it. We can be sensitive to the unction of the Holy Spirit. He may lead in a different direction. There may be someone in need who is not on the list but suddenly the names comes to mind so you pray for that person. Or the Holy Spirit may lead you to spend the entire time praying in tongues. The prayer list, however, will make prayer time more structured when the Spirit does not lead in a different direction.

When I begin praying I pray for the leaders of the nation and other countries first. I follow by praying for those who are in the ministry; next, my church family; lastly my family and myself. Most of the time I never get to me. This does not mean that I pray this way every day; however, if the Spirit does not change my direction, this is the general structure. I also spend much of my prayer time praying in tongues.

Pray in the Spirit

¹⁴For if I pray in an [unknown] tongue, my spirit [by the Holy Spirit within me] prays, but my mind is unproductive [it bears no fruit and helps nobody]. ¹⁵Then what am I to do? I will pray with my spirit [by the Holy Spirit that is within me], but I will also pray [intelligently] with my mind and understanding; I will sing with my spirit [by the Holy Spirit that is within me], but I will sing [intelligently] with my mind and understanding also.

1 Corinthians 14:14,15 (AMP)

Praying in the Spirit is praying in tongues. When we pray in tongues it should be done in private because we are speaking directly to God. Only God understands what we are saying. He gives us a language to communicate with Him from our spirits and it bypasses the intellect. We can pray in tongues about things that cannot be put in words to tell the Father.

We cannot understand what is being said, but God knows. He knows the thoughts and intents of the heart. As we pray in tongues, it is the Spirit in control of the prayer. One of the great advantages of praying in the Holy Ghost is that Satan cannot understand what we are saying to God and, therefore, cannot hinder it.

For he that speaketh in an *unknown* tongue speaketh not unto men, but unto God: for no man understandeth *him*; howbeit in the spirit he speaketh mysteries.
1 Corinthians 14:2 (KJV)

Here again Paul explains that we are talking directly to God and that mysteries are revealed. I urge all Christians to spend time in prayer, especially praying in tongues. By doing so, revelation and direction will come for your future, your marriage, your children, your ministry, your business or your job. God will show exactly what you need to do.

Every believer should spend time with God praying in the spirit so they will always know what God has in store. God will show specific directions if we give Him the opportunity. One of the great things about prayer is that not only are we talking to God, He talks to us!

Prayer is like focusing the lens of a camera on the object being photographed. The object should be clear, not fuzzy or distorted. As the lens is turned to the right setting, the object becomes focused and the photo is taken. When we pray in the Spirit, the direction for the day, week, month and even for life becomes clearer. We receive strength to be able to go in the direction that God has for us. We are built up in the faith so we can stand against the attacks of the enemy and be an overcomer in everything.

But ye, beloved, building up yourselves on your most holy faith, praying in the Holy Ghost...
Jude 1:20 (KJV)

The Spirit helps our weaknesses and makes intercession for us. There are times when we don't know how to pray concerning a situation, but the Holy Spirit knows exactly what to say. When we pray in tongues, the Spirit prays or says things that we can't put into words. There are times when we are praying for others and really don't know how to pray for them. Praying in tongues overrides our lack of knowledge and the Spirit does what we wanted to do but couldn't.

> **Likewise the Spirit also helpeth our infirmities: for we know not what we should pray for as we ought: but the Spirit itself maketh intercession for us with groanings which cannot be uttered.**
>
> **Romans 8:26 (KJV)**

Pray without ceasing

We are further admonished by Paul in 1 Thessalonians 5:17 to pray without ceasing. This is done by beginning the day with individual prayer and intercession, praying in tongues at every opportunity, rejoicing in spiritual songs and hymns, praying a prayer of agreement with someone, attending intercession at church, entering into a united prayer, or maybe choosing to spend the day in prayer and fasting. The believer looks for every opportunity to pray.

> **Pray at all times (on every occasion, in every season) in the Spirit, with all [manner of] prayer and entreaty. To that end keep alert and watch with strong purpose and perseverance, interceding in behalf of all the saints (God's consecrated people).**
>
> **Ephesians 6:18 (AMP)**

Paul exhorts us to pray at all times and with all manner of prayers. He is actually saying to pray the type of prayer that is needed for a specific need or time—whether it be a prayer of request (Mark 11:24), a united prayer (Acts 4:31-33), a prayer of worship and praise (Acts 13:2), the prayer of intercession (Romans 8:26) or a special time set aside for fasting and prayer (Matthew 17:20,21).

Paul is also saying we are not to pray for ourselves only, but to pray for others as well. We are to be sensitive to the needs of others so we can pray with all perseverance until we see the need met.

Fasting

Fasting should become a part of the life of a Christian—not out of obligation, but out of a desire to hear God's voice. To clarify, let me say that fasting will not grant the answer to prayers, force God to move or give a believer more power. Fasting and prayer together help quiet the mind and body so the voice of the Spirit can be heard more clearly, more easily. Faith will bring the answer and believers always have power. Fasting is one of the ways to use that power.

Fasting does not draw us closer to God. When we were born again, we were as close as we will ever get. But as our minds are renewed and we fully understand righteousness, we become more conscious of the God who lives within each of us.

Fasting should be done in private. It should not be something that we tell people we are doing.

17 But thou, when thou fastest, anoint thine head, and wash thy face; 18 That thou appear not unto men to fast, but unto thy Father which is in secret: and thy Father, which seeth in secret, shall reward thee openly.
Matthew 6:17,18 (KJV)

We are not to have a sad countenance when fasting so that others would look upon us. This is between the believer and the Lord.

To fast one, three, five or even seven days there need not be a special leading from God. However, there should be a purpose in the fast—a need for direction or a situation that requires clarification. Don't fast just to be fasting. An extended fast, I believe, should be followed only when there is a specific direction from the Lord. When Jesus fasted forty days He was led by the Spirit.

> **Then was Jesus led up of the Spirit into the wilderness to be tempted of the devil. And when he had fasted forty days and forty nights, he was afterward an hungered.**
> **Matthew 4:1,2 (KJV)**

Jesus was led by the Spirit to do so and we should follow His example.

When operating in the ministry gift of an evangelist, I have spent much time in prayer and fasting. I have fasted as long as forty days, but it was through the direction of the Holy Spirit. On many occasions I have been led to fast twenty-one days, fourteen days, ten days and so on, but God led me to do so. During those times my mind and body became so tuned to God that great revivals and miracles took place.

It was not the fasting that brought the power, but fasting calmed my body and quieted my mind so God's voice was clearer and as I yielded to Him, He manifested His power.

I trust that I've said something in this chapter that will inspire all Christians to pray more. I love to pray and cherish each moment that I have alone in my prayer closet. I enjoy the times of prayer with other people and riding in my car praying in tongues. However, the time when I shut the door in the morning and am alone with God is what I look forward to most in life. Remember...

> **...the effectual fervent prayer of a righteous man availeth much.**
> **James 5:16 (KJV)**

Chapter 11
Fellowship

Fellowship with God and fellowship with other believers are important to every believer's spiritual growth. These two types of fellowship go hand in hand.

Believers fellowship with God through prayer, meditating in the Word and praying in the spirit. But we also fellowship with Him when we spend time with other believers.

When we gather with other believers, Jesus is there with us. **For where two or three gather together because they are mine, I am there among them." Matthew 18:20 (NLT)**

When we join to fellowship with the Father and His Son, we are also joined in a special partnership, or fellowship with one another.

What we have seen and [ourselves] heard, we are also telling you, so that you too may realize and enjoy fellowship as partners and partakers with us. And [this] fellowship that we have [which is a distinguishing mark of Christians] is with the Father and with His Son Jesus Christ (the Messiah).

1 John 1:3 (AMP)

Fellowship defined

Webster defined *fellowship* as "the condition of being an associate; mutual association of persons on equal and friendly terms; communion; companionship; intimate familiarity, a mutual sharing, partnership or joint interest."

Fellowship with the Lord

Fellowship with the Lord involves being on friendly terms, communing (talking, communicating) with Him, knowing Him intimately, being companions, inviting His presence and participation in all you do, sharing your love and all you are with Him just as He shares His love and all that He is with you.

The scriptures make it clear that God desires fellowship with man. He fellowshipped with Adam in the garden. He lived in close fellowship with Enoch (Genesis 5). He had a close relationship with Noah (Genesis 6:9). He fellowshipped and ate with Abraham (Genesis 18). He promised Moses, "I will personally go with you Moses." (Exodus 33:14). He called Moses His friend (Exodus 33:17). And Jesus spent 33 years on this earth involved in the lives of people.

Communion, or The Lord's Supper

In the New Testament we find the Lord's Supper, or the serving of Communion, described as a time of fellowship—with the Lord and with other believers. When Jesus shared the "Last Supper" with his disciples, it was a time of fellowship with the Father and with one another. The very word we have ascribed to this celebration, "Communion," denotes that it is a time of fellowship.

They joined with the other believers and devoted themselves to the apostles' teaching and fellowship, sharing in the Lord's Supper and in prayer.

Acts 2:42 (NLT)

⁴⁶They worshiped together at the Temple each day, met in homes for the Lord's Supper, and shared their meals with great joy and generosity—⁴⁷all the while praising God and enjoying the goodwill of all the people. And each day the Lord added to their group those who were being saved.

Acts 2:46,47 (NLT)

Other references

The many references to man's fellowship with God in both the Old and New Testaments show that God desires a personal and intimate relationship with us. We learn that as believers we are sisters and brothers of Jesus and share the same Father. Of course, this makes us sisters and brothers to each other. We are a family and have the marvelous opportunity to have a truly personal relationship with our Father, our Lord Jesus and the Holy Spirit—and each other. Here are just a few of those scriptures:

Jesus answered, If a person [really] loves Me, he will keep My word [obey My teaching]; and My Father will love him, and We will come to him and make Our home (abode, special dwelling place) with him.

John 14:23 (AMP)

⁸He will keep you strong to the end, so that you will be blameless on the day of our Lord Jesus Christ. ⁹God, who has called you into fellowship with his Son Jesus Christ our Lord, is faithful.

1 Corinthians 1:8,9 (NIV)

The amazing grace of the Master, Jesus Christ, the extravagant love of God, the intimate friendship of the Holy Spirit, be with all of you.

2 Corinthians 13:14 (TMNT)

[10]I want to know Christ and the power of his resurrection and the fellowship of sharing in his sufferings, becoming like him in his death, [11]and so, somehow, to attain to the resurrection from the dead.

Philippians 3:10,11 (NIV)

[11]So now Jesus and the ones he makes holy have the same Father. That is why Jesus is not ashamed to call them his brothers and sisters. [12]For he said to God, "I will declare the wonder of your name to my brothers and sisters. I will praise you among all your people."

Hebrews 2:11,12 (NLT)

What we have seen and [ourselves] heard, we are also telling you, so that you too may realize and enjoy fellowship as partners and partakers with us. And [this] fellowship that we have [which is a distinguishing mark of Christians] is with the Father and with His Son Jesus Christ (the Messiah).

1 John 1:3 (AMP)

[24]So you must remain faithful to what you have been taught from the beginning. If you do, you will continue to live in fellowship with the Son and with the Father. [25]And in this fellowship we enjoy the eternal life he promised us.

1 John 2:24,25 (NLT)

And now, dear children, continue to live in fellowship with Christ so that when he returns, you will be full of courage and not shrink back from him in shame.

1 John 2:28 (NLT)

Walking in obedience is a must...

Those who obey God's commandments live in fellowship with him, and he with them. And we know he lives in us because the Holy Spirit lives in us.

1 John 3:24 (NLT)

For if you wander beyond the teaching of Christ, you will not have fellowship with God. But if you continue in the teaching of Christ, you will have fellowship with both the Father and the Son.

2 John 1:9 (NLT)

I do not have fellowship with tricky, two-faced men; they are false and hypocritical.

Psalm 26:4 (TLB)

What a blessing!

What an awesome privilege and blessing—that the Almighty God, creator of all that is, desires a personal relationship with each of us. His desire for this is so great that Jesus suffered and died to make it possible!

Receiving Jesus as Lord and Savior opens the door for this marvelous fellowship.

**"Look! I have been standing at the door, and I am
constantly knocking. If anyone hears me calling him and
opens the door, I will come in and fellowship with him
and he with me.**

Revelation 3:20 (TLB)

Fellowship with the Lord is such an awesome privilege, and yet so
often we ignore Him! We get busy "doing" and fail to spend quality time
talking to Him and listening to Him and getting better acquainted with
Him through His Word.

Some ways to fellowship with the Lord:

- Time in your prayer closet—away from distractions
- Praying and singing in the spirit
- "Chatting" with Him as you go about your day
- Meditating on His Word
- Taking communion
- Worshipping with other believers
- Sharing goals and plans—make His goals your goals, His desires
  your desires

Fellowship with God because that is His desire. Fellowship with God
because you love Him and want to spend time with Him. Fellowship with
God so that you will grow to know Him better and serve Him more.
Fellowship with God so that you may be victorious in all you do.

**And a second reminder, dear children: You know the
Father from personal experience. You veterans know the
One who started it all; and you newcomers—such vitality
and strength! God's word is so steady in you. Your
fellowship with God enables you to gain a victory over
the Evil One.**

1 John 2:14 (TMNT)

Fellowship with other believers

The word *fellowship* comes from the Greek word *koinonia*, which involves associating, participating, communicating, an interchange of ideas. When we fellowship with other members in the body of Christ we should associate, communicate, participate, cooperate, edify and celebrate.

Where to fellowship

Fellowship can be at church or other places, but church should be the first priority. Every believer needs to be actively involved in a church. Every believer needs a pastor in addition to fellowship with the saints.

Don't let Satan or circumstances keep you from attending church regularly. The Word says not to forsake the assembling of ourselves together.

Let's see how inventive we can be in encouraging love and helping out, not avoiding worshiping together as some do but spurring each other on, especially as we see the big Day approaching.
Hebrews 10:24,25 (TMNT)

Fellowship within the church can be during worship service, in smaller classes such as Sunday school, at prayer meetings, at work meetings, going together on outreach projects, doing volunteer work of any kind, at social gatherings—anywhere you are participating or communicating with other believers. It can even be walking or riding together to church—as in the case of David and his companion.

Instead, it is you—my equal, my companion and close friend. What good fellowship we enjoyed as we walked together to the house of God.
Psalm 55:13,14 (NLT)

Although some of your closest relationships should be with people in your church, do not limit yourself to that. Fellowship with other believers in many ways—at home, at social events and at recreational activities. Invite one another over for a meal—or just a fun time to talk or play games or watch a sports event on television. Go on picnics and other outings together. Stay in touch by phone or e-mail. Baby-sit for each other. Pray together and discuss what new things you are learning from God's Word and your walk with Him. Share your struggles and your needs. In other words, share your lives.

Fellowship should not be limited to people from your church. Every believer in the world is part of your family! Be open to fellowshipping with Christians from other churches, other denominations, other cultures, and even other countries.

Encourage each other

Encouraging one another is one part of fellowship. A classic example is found in 1 Samuel. Jonathan and David were the closest of friends—and they recognized the importance of encouraging each other.

> **Jonathan went to find David and encouraged him to stay strong in his faith in God.**
> **1 Samuel 23:16 (NLT)**

In order to encourage each other, we have to stay in touch. Be aware of what's happening with others. Don't get so focused on your own needs or so busy in your day-to-day activities that you ignore your brothers' and sisters' needs. Stay involved with each other!

> **[11]For I long to visit you so I can share a spiritual blessing with you that will help you grow strong in the Lord. [12]I'm eager to encourage you in your faith, but I**

also want to be encouraged by yours. In this way, each of us will be a blessing to the other.

Romans 1:11,12 (NLT)

So let's agree to use all our energy in getting along with each other. Help others with encouraging words; don't drag them down by finding fault..

Romans 14:19 (TMNT)

Therefore encourage one another and build each other up, just as in fact you are doing.

1 Thessalonians 5:11 (NIV)

Pray for each other

Along with encouragement comes prayer. In your private prayer time, pray for other believers. Be involved in their lives enough that you can pray specifically.

And sometimes when you are together, pray for others and for each other.

If someone is pouring out their heart to you, don't limit yourself to just saying "I'll pray for you" (although this is good to do). Be sensitive to God's leading, and if it seems right, be bold and caring enough to take their hand and pray with them right then!

The early church fellowshipped and prayed for each other...

They all met together continually for prayer, along with Mary the mother of Jesus, several other women, and the brothers of Jesus.

Acts 1:14 (NLT)

They joined with the other believers and devoted themselves to the apostles' teaching and fellowship, sharing in the Lord's Supper and in prayer.

Acts 2:42 (NLT)

And so should we…

Therefore confess your sins to each other and pray for each other so that you may be healed. The prayer of a righteous man is powerful and effective.

James 5:16 (NIV)

Spiritual fellowship

Along with praying together come singing praises, sharing testimonies, any way of honoring God together.

[19]Talk with each other much about the Lord, quoting psalms and hymns and singing sacred songs, making music in your hearts to the Lord. [20]Always give thanks for everything to our God and Father in the name of our Lord Jesus Christ.

Ephesians 5:19,20 (TLB)

Share one another's joys and sorrows

An important part of fellowship includes showing genuine concern for each other, loving one another in action as well as word. It's easy to say, "I love you." But the words are meaningless unless our actions demonstrate that love.

When you learn that a fellow believer is in need, what do you do about it? Do you really care about those things that concern others? Do you really joy in their victories? Those things are all part of fellowship—part of God's plan for every member of His family.

> [44]And all the believers met together constantly and shared everything they had. [45]They sold their possessions and shared the proceeds with those in need. [46]They worshiped together at the Temple each day, met in homes for the Lord's Supper, and shared their meals with great joy and generosity— [47]all the while praising God and enjoying the goodwill of all the people. And each day the Lord added to their group those who were being saved.
>
> Acts 2:44-47 (NLT)

> [15]When others are happy, be happy with them. If they are sad, share their sorrow. [16]Work happily together. Don't try to act big. Don't try to get into the good graces of important people, but enjoy the company of ordinary folks. And don't think you know it all!
>
> Romans 12:15,16 (TLB)

> Those of us who are strong and able in the faith need to step in and lend a hand to those who falter, and not just do what is most convenient for us. Strength is for service, not status. Each one of us needs to look after the good of the people around us, asking ourselves, "How can I help?"
>
> That's exactly what Jesus did. He didn't make it easy for himself by avoiding people's troubles, but waded right in and helped out. "I took on the troubles of the troubled," is the way Scripture puts it. Even if it was written in Scripture long ago, you can be sure it's written for us. God wants the combination of his steady, constant calling and warm, personal counsel in Scripture to come to characterize us, keeping us alert for whatever he will do

next. May our dependably steady and warmly personal God develop maturity in you so that you get along with each other as well as Jesus gets along with us all. Then we'll be a choir—not our voices only, but our very lives singing in harmony in a stunning anthem to the God and Father of our Master Jesus!

Romans 15:1-6 (TMNT)

Share each other's troubles and problems, and in this way obey the law of Christ.

Galatians 6:2 (NLT)

[10]Whenever we have the opportunity, we should do good to everyone, especially to our Christian brothers and sisters.

Galatians 6:10 (NLT)

Serving Him together

Fellowship includes sharing common goals and purpose and joining together to accomplish those things.

As believers we have many common purposes—honoring God, spreading the gospel, building up the body of Christ, and being salt and light to the world. God has blessed us each with special talents and gifts to prepare us for our role in the body. It is so important that each of us recognizes what part God has given us and do it wholeheartedly unto Him. It is also important that we recognize and appreciate the special part He has given to each other believer and that we respect and support one another in these roles.

⁴Just as our bodies have many parts and each part has a special function, ⁵so it is with Christ's body. We are all parts of his one body, and each of us has different work to do. And since we are all one body in Christ, we belong to each other, and each of us needs all the others.

Romans 12:4,5 (NLT)

Let the peace of Christ keep you in tune with each other, in step with each other. None of this going off and doing your own thing. And cultivate thankfulness. Let the Word of Christ—the Message—have the run of the house. Give it plenty of room in your lives. Instruct and direct one another using good common sense. And sing, sing your hearts out to God! Let every detail in your lives— words, actions, whatever—be done in the name of the Master, Jesus, thanking God the Father every step of the way.

Colossians 3:15-17 (TMNT)

Get along among yourselves, each of you doing your part. Our counsel is that you warn the freeloaders to get a move on. Gently encourage the stragglers, and reach out for the exhausted, pulling them to their feet. Be patient with each person, attentive to individual needs. And be careful that when you get on each other's nerves you don't snap at each other. Look for the best in each other, and always do your best to bring it out.

1 Thessalonians 5:14,15 (TMNT)

Living in harmony and love

Jesus said that our love for each other is what will set us apart. When others see that love, they will know that we belong to Him.

³⁴**So now I am giving you a new commandment: Love each other. Just as I have loved you, you should love each other.** ³⁵**Your love for one another will prove to the world that you are my disciples."**

John 13:34,35 (NLT)

Does the world see this kind of love in our lives?

When we take offense because someone has been short with us or didn't meet our expectation in some way—is that love?

When we blindly insist on our own way in a relationship or a church program or decision—is that love?

When we expect people to be interested in our problems but never even consider theirs—is that love?

When we gossip about each other (sometimes even disguising the gossip as "prayer requests")—is that love?

When we get mad and leave a church because everything isn't going our way—is that love?

If you've gotten anything at all out of following Christ, if his love has made any difference in your life, if being in a community of the Spirit means anything to you, if you have a heart, if you care—then do me a favor: Agree with each other, love each other, be deep-spirited friends. Don't push your way to the front; don't sweet-talk your way to the top. Put yourself aside, and help others get ahead. Don't be obsessed with getting your own advantage. Forget yourselves long enough to lend a helping hand.

Philippians 2:1-4 (TMNT)

I have a serious concern to bring up with you, my friends, using the authority of Jesus, our Master. I'll put it as urgently as I can: You *must* get along with each other. You must learn to be considerate of one another, cultivating a life in common.

1 Corinthians 1:10 (TMNT)

Stay on good terms with each other, held together by love.

Hebrews 3:1 (TMNT)

Summing up: Be agreeable, be sympathetic, be loving, be compassionate, be humble. That goes for all of you, no exceptions. No retaliation. No sharp-tongued sarcasm. Instead, bless—that's your job, to bless. You'll be a blessing and also get a blessing.

1 Peter 3:8-9 (TMNT)

Fellowshipping with other believers by demonstrating our love to them comes from fellowshipping with the Father.

[11]Dear friends, since God loved us as much as that, we surely ought to love each other too. [12]For though we have never yet seen God, when we love each other God lives in us, and his love within us grows ever stronger. [13]And he has put his own Holy Spirit into our hearts as a proof to us that we are living with him and he with us.

1 John 4:11-13 (TLB)

Believers walking in sin

God's Word gives some very specific instruction regarding our relationship with believers who are willfully living in sin. We cannot truly fellowship with them—they are not walking in obedience and their fellowship with the Father has been interrupted. And so our relationship has to change—at least for now. Instead of praying with them, we will pray for them. We have a responsibility to do what we can to help this family member get back on track.

> ... you shouldn't act as if everything is just fine when one of your Christian companions is promiscuous or crooked, is flip with God or rude to friends, gets drunk or becomes greedy and predatory. You can't just go along with this, treating it as acceptable behavior. I'm not responsible for what the *outsiders* do, but don't we have some responsibility for those within our community of believers? God decides on the outsiders, but we need to decide when our brothers and sisters are out of line and, if necessary, clean house.
>
> 1 Corinthians 5:11-13 (TMNT)

> Dear brothers and sisters, if another Christian is overcome by some sin, you who are godly should gently and humbly help that person back onto the right path. And be careful not to fall into the same temptation yourself.
>
> Galatians 6:1 (NLT)

What about unbelievers?

What about unbelievers? Should we fellowship with them?

No, not in the same sense that we do with believers. We don't share the same life goals and guidelines. We can't share worship time. We cannot work together to accomplish the purpose of our God-given journey...but we should spend time with them.

Jesus said we are to be in the world but not of the world. We are not to join the world's ways or be defined by the world. But we are to be in the world and bring light into it (John 17:13-19 TMNT)

Jesus was criticized again and again for spending time with sinners. His answer? That's who He came to save!

Later Jesus and his disciples were at home having supper with a collection of disreputable guests. Unlikely as it seems, more than a few of them had become followers. The religion scholars and Pharisees saw him keeping this kind of company and lit into his disciples: "What kind of example is this, acting cozy with the riffraff?"

Jesus, overhearing, shot back, "Who needs a doctor: the healthy or the sick? I'm here inviting the sin-sick, not the spiritually-fit."

Mark 2:15-17 (TMNT)

Jesus has called us to be salt and light. In order to do that, we need to spend time with people who are not yet saved.

"Let me tell you why you are here. You're here to be salt-seasoning that brings out the God-flavors of this earth. If you lose your saltiness, how will people taste godliness? You've lost your usefulness and will end up in the garbage.

"Here's another way to put it: You're here to be light, bringing out the God-colors in the world. God is not a secret to be kept. We're going public with this, as public as a city on a hill. If I make you light-bearers, you don't think I'm going to hide you under a bucket, do you? I'm putting you on a light stand. Now that I've put you there on a hilltop, on a light stand—shine! Keep open house;

be generous with your lives. By opening up to others, you'll prompt people to open up with God, this generous Father in heaven.

Matthew 5:13-16 (TMNT)

It is essential for us to spend time with family, friends, co-workers and others who are not saved. How else can we bring the gospel to them? However, there are important things to remember.

Take care that you are influencing them by your lifestyle, not the other way around. It has been said that if you are standing on a chair, it is easier for someone on the ground to pull you down than for you to pull him or her up.

Stay in prayer. Whenever appropriate, try to have another believer join you in the time spent with unbelievers. Maintain fellowship with your Father and with other believers.

Paul says it well...

...Go out into the world uncorrupted, a breath of fresh air in this squalid and polluted society. Provide people with a glimpse of good living and of the living God. Carry the light-giving Message into the night so I'll have good cause to be proud of you on the day that Christ returns. You'll be living proof that I didn't go to all this work for nothing.

Philippians 2:14-16 (TMNT)

A necessary ingredient

And so we see that fellowship is at the very core of our growth to spiritual maturity. Fellowship with our Lord. Fellowship with believers.

God has a mission for each of us—let us encourage each other, help each other and pray for each other as we move along the road to accomplish His purpose for us.

In light of all this, here's what I want you to do. While I'm locked up here, a prisoner for the Master, I want you to get out there and walk—better yet, run!—on the road God called you to travel. I don't want any of you sitting around on your hands. I don't want anyone strolling off, down some path that goes nowhere. And mark that you do this with humility and discipline—not in fits and starts, but steadily, pouring yourselves out for each other in acts of love, alert at noticing differences and quick at mending fences.

You were all called to travel on the same road and in the same direction, so stay together, both outwardly and inwardly. You have one Master, one faith, one baptism, one God and Father of all, who rules over all, works through all, and is present in all. Everything you are and think and do is permeated with Oneness.

Ephesians 1-6 (TMNT)

In conclusion…

I have not intended for the different chapters in this book to be consecutive steps into spiritual maturity. Growing into maturity is more of a process of incorporating each area into our daily lives. Each of us has weak areas and stronger areas. As you read and study this book and the scriptures it suggests, I exhort you to find the places where you may fall short…and fill them.

This book has not just been taken from messages that I have preached and later transcribed. I have taken the time to sit down and put myself into these pages—to share parts of my life, both mistakes and victories. I trust that showing where I have been and where I am now demonstrates the maturing process. My life is now what it is because I have learned to be patient. This growth does not come overnight—it is a continual developmental process. One thing is for sure—I will continue growing!

I believe that as you apply the simple truths that lie in these pages, you too will continue to grow and mature to be more like Jesus.

Other Books
by
Don Clowers

·Spiritual Growth Study Guide
(Companion to this book)

• God's Prescription for Health and Healing

• God's Prescription for Health and Healing Study Guide

• Right and Wrong Expectations in Friendship

• Never Be A Victim Again

• Never Be A Victim Again Study Guide

• The Power of Hope

• The Power of Hope Study Guide

• Show Me…How To Find More Meaning in My Life

Contact Us

e-mail <u>dcm@donclowers.com</u>
web site <u>www.donclowers.com</u>

United States
Don Clowers Ministries
P.O. Box 3168
Coppell, TX 75019
(972) 258-6525
fax 800 506-6736

Canada
Don Clowers Evangelistic Association of Canada
4261-A14 Hwy. 7, Suite 243
Markham, ON L3R-9W6

Philippines
Don Clowers Ministries Philippines
P.O. Box 1496
1000 Manila